BASIC SURF

About the Author 2
Introduction 4
History of Surfing 5
Part One — Beginning S
Beach Preparation 7
Paddling Through Surf 10
Traffic in the Surf 13
Wave Directions 15
Riding White Water 17
Catching a Wave 19
Beginning Rides 23
Rules of the Road 26
Advice on Wipeouts 26
Hazards of the Surf 28
Part Two — Surfing Maneuvers
Surfing Theory 32
Introduction to Maneuvering 34
Bottom Turn, Top Turn 35
Turn Back and "S" Maneuver 38
Trimming and Stalling 41
Nose Rides and Fin Releases 45
Kick Out, Roller Coaster 48
Curl Rides 51
Backside Approach **54,56**
Climb and Drop Approach **41,55**
Right Wave Complete 57
Left Wave Complete 60
Other Maneuvers 63
Advice on Maneuvering 65
Maneuvering in Contests 66
Riding Big Surf 67
Approach to Pipelines 73
Part Three — Wave Formation
Beaches, Points and Reefs 77
Jetties, Piers and River Mouths 80
Tides and Swells 85
Weather and Swells 87
Seasons and Surf 89
Part Four — Surfing Equipment
Surfboard Descriptions 90
Surfboard Designs 92
Surfboard Transport, Care & Repair 96
Wetsuits — Care and Repair 98

Colorful Surfing Terminology 101
The Living Curl, The Californians 106

ABOUT THE AUTHOR

Jamie Budge began surfing in 1960 after catching his first wave by mistake on a long hollow paddleboard. The next day he bought his first real surfboard and has been surfing consistently ever since. He has been involved in every aspect of the sport, including competing in contests, staging contests, designing and making surfboards, producing and lecturing with surf films, making TV and radio appearances. Jamie has accumulated over twenty trophies from competitions on both the west and east coasts including the Atlantic States Surfing Championships. And as a result of the Morey Noserider Pro Championships in 1966, Jamie was the 5th rated professional surfer in California (for a while).

Announcing the Smirnoff Invitational Surfing Champions in Santa Cruz, circa 1970,
Photo: Hal Jepson

Surfing at Leo Carrillo State Beach in the 1976 Oarhouse Longboard Surfing Contest.
Photo: David Mellin

For several years, Jamie filmed and produced surfing movies, and has made three complete lecture tours along the coasts of the continental United States. Jamie was twice the guest star of Stan Richard's "Surf's Up" TV show and was the host/announcer of the TV special of the 1970 United States Surfing Championships held at Huntington Beach. And Jamie was President of the prestigious Malibu Surfing Association. His latest involvement in the sport (as of 1970) was the teaching of surfing classes at Pepperdine University in Malibu, California. It was these classes that inspired compiling his 12 years of experience and observations into this book.

After 8 years of non-stop activity (since the age of 16) Jamie had "retired" from all things serious in surfing by the time he was 24. But he sill announced the ocassional surfing contest. And placed 9th in a Longboard Invitational contest (of the top 200 surfers of the '60's) at Malibu.

About the Author

And got 3rd Place and "Best Ride of the Day" a the Oarhouse Longboard Contest in the mid-'70's judged by Lance Carson at Leo Carrillo State Beach (Sequit),

Jamie pursued his film-making career by making promotional films about new sports such as windsurfing, hang-gliding, inline skating and skateboarding (with the new urethane wheels). As an offshoot of the new sports, Jamie came up with his own alternative sport, which he called "WindSkating": a sail on a skateboard (and later roller skates).

In the late '70's and into the '80's, WindSkating became a popular media hit and was featured in magazines and newspapers around the world, as well as TV commercials, news programs, television and short subject and feature length movies.

Test driving the original WindSkate prototype circa 1974. photo: Craig Stecyk

Jamie found WindSkating a welcome alternative to ever-more-crowded sport of surfing. And he pioneered the development of the skate sailing around the world: selling thousands of WindSkates in the process.

The popularity of WindSkates in the media led Jamie back to another love: photography. During the '80's and '90's, Jamie produced and photographed action stunts and human interest features for publications around the world, including the National Enquirer and Star Magazines here in the United States.

Over the years (well, decades) Jamie had ignored requests to release his surf films on DVD (mainly because the technology wasn't ready for them yet). But in 2008, Jamie released "The Living Curl" on DVD and later "The Californians" (in 2010). As well as resurrecting personally live-narrated showings at events in California.

Due to the overwhelmingly postitive reception of the DVD's, Jamie also pulled "Basic Surfing" off the shelf.

And here it is, for your education and entertainment . . .

INTRODUCTION

Surfing is a fascinating sport because it looks so easy when performed by the experienced surfer. The surfers movements look spontaneous and in complete harmony with the wave he is riding. The illusion is one of a carefree and joyous ride over the sparkling swells of nature. But, as in a well performed ballet, this is the result of years of practice and careful study.

The following hundred-plus pages is an outline of the knowledge that every experienced surfer has accumulated in order to achieve that carefree and joyous ride. We hope that this book will be a guide to many beginning surfers as they go through the awkward stages of learning. We might also hope to refresh some of those experienced surfers who have always known, but weren't too sure what it was that they have known. But whatever your experience with surfing, we want you to enjoy the book as well as give credit to those who have dedicated years to mastering the sport of surfing.

When one starts surfing, the first thing he notices is that there is enough going on out there to fill a book. But because every surfer assumes that he and everybody else knows everything there is to know, these books never get written. At least they never get written in a form that the average individual can understand without an experienced surfing interpreter. So the theory behind this book is to take the occurrences in surfing that seem so obvious that they never get explained, and explain them. The hope would be that this book would guide many beginning surfers through all those awkward stages of not knowing what is going on until it is absorbed through experience. We might also hope to pick up some of those "experienced" surfers who might want to take a look at what they always have known, but haven't known exactly what it is that they've known. If this book gets too complex, look at the pictures and cartoons. And we hope that this book will be as much fun to read as it was to compile.

The Author

SURFING HISTORY

The sport of surfing is recorded as far back as the discovery of the Hawaiian Islands by Captain Cook in the 17th century. At that time Captain Cook noted in his ship's journal that the local natives held a form of athletic games in which riding the waves from far out at sea to the beach was a part. The actual type of boards that these natives used is somewhat speculative, but the older relics of the earliest surfboards are extremely long (20 ft.) and of very heavy hardwood (over one hundred pounds). Part of the measure of masculinity was based on being able to carry one of these boards down to the surf. If one were courageous enough to get that far, then the surf would probably give him little trouble.

Surfing was somewhat refined during the 1930's and boards were a little shorter and lighter due to lighter woods and hollow boards. But these boards worked best in the long rolling swells of Hawaiian waves. Riding one was sort of like setting a course on the Queen Mary: once you set your direction you did not want to change it for minor obstacles or major surf. After World War II, more refinements were made when surfing was introduced to California. The long heavy board worked well only at a few select locations, and the Californians were quick to instigate some new designs.

Balsa Wood became more of a standard for surfboards because it could be shaped to certain specifications and curved contours. It was about this time, toward the late 1950's, that surfers discovered they could turn these boards in different directions on the face of the wave and make them go faster or slower with weight shifting. And later in the early 1960's when foam and fiberglass became standard materials, these boards were reduced to 9 to 10 ft. and about 25 lbs. in weight.

These boards and Gidget turned the sport of surfing into an over-night coastal sensation. There were surf heroes, surf cars, surfing movies, surf girls, surf radio, and all the accessories that anyone could put "surf" in front of. Surfing maneuvers were invented, practiced, refined and instigated into newly formed surfing contests. Surfing clubs and surfing associations sprang up throughout the United States, and international affiliations were formed.

This trend in surfing lasted till about 1966 when the Australians introduced the "short board" to the Californians. These boards were dropping the standard length down to 7 ft. and the weight down to close to 10 lbs. And with these boards came a new aggressive style of surfing to which imagination seemed the only limit.

Surfing History

Surfers could ride up, down, back, forth, off the bottom, through the top, inside and outside, all within the space of a few seconds. Surfing purists were born to whom the only object of surfing was the ultimate wave, board design and lack of crowds. Much of the fad element fell away, and the remaining enthusiasts were much more concerned. And from these more recent changes seems to have developed an internationally recognized and respected sporting activity of the 1980's — Surfing.

BEACH PREPARATION

Although "Preparation on the Beach" may seem like a ridiculous point to an experienced surfer, there is still a process and evaluation that every surfer goes through before entering the water. To begin with, one must rub wax on the top or deck of the surfboard. When applied to a clean or new board, the wax will rub on in a thin coat and begin to build up ridges and nodules (lumps and bumps) that will be your only foot traction on a wet surfboard. This is essential for any surfing. Old wax bumps can be re-waxed for new traction every time a surfer re-enters the water. It is also a little known fact that a standard plastic comb is one of the best tools for putting a new non-slip surface on old wax.

All dings should be repaired (see chapter on surfboard care and repair). An un-repaired ding will have loose fibreglass and dented foam which can be very unpleasant to the bare skin. An unrepaired ding will also cause the surfboard to take on weight, as the board soaks up water into the foam (called "water-logged"; do not buy a surfboard in this condition.) If one does not have enough time to repair the ding with putty and fibreglass, at least seal it with plastic tape to keep it from taking on water.

There are also several conditions that a beginning surfer should avoid. These would be: extremely large surf, with large crowds to match, completely deserted beaches (which may have good reasons for being so), surfing through piers, over large submerged rocks or shallow reefs; surfing with a full stomach, which may precede extreme cramps; and an obvious list including sharks, lightning bolts, rip tides, maelstroms, etc. All of these factors, combined or individually, may have no effect in deterring the experienced, or fanatical, surfer, but a beginner should start with milder conditions.

Choosing a course through the surf is the next step. At an average beach break, the surfers will usually cluster around various peaks for the most advantageous take-off point. A surfer should usually find a route in between these clusters and surf breaks to paddle out to the takeoff points himself. At a point break, the waves will wrap in long lines around the point, breaking mostly in one direction, usually to the right. The easiest route is usually through the cove (where the waves are smaller and closer to the shore) and then out and around the line-up of surf and surfers to an advantageous take-off point (which is mostly just an un-crowded section of wave).

If this route seems a long paddle, then a surfer might walk along the beach out to the point itself before entering the water. This is accompanied by a short paddle, which must be done quickly,

PREPARATION ON BEACH

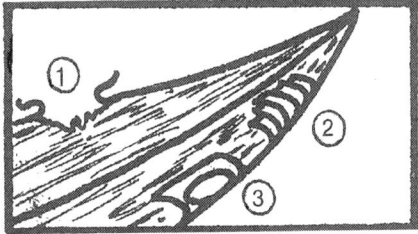

WAXING YOUR BOARD with parafin wax forms ridges on top board for foot traction.
DINGS SHOULD BE REPAIRED
1. New ding 2. Ding taped to seal from water. 3. Ding repaired with putty & glass.

BEACH BREAK — Surf breaks in shifting peaks. Find route thru surf avoiding breaking waves and other surfers.

POINT BREAK — Surf breaks in long lines wrapping around the point. Take long easy route thru cove and around line up or short fast route between surf and surfers.

REEF BREAK — Usually breaks in one pronounced peak. Paddle around either side of this peak to take off point.

Beach Preparation . . .

Author Jamie Budge waxes up his transistional short board, circa 1970.

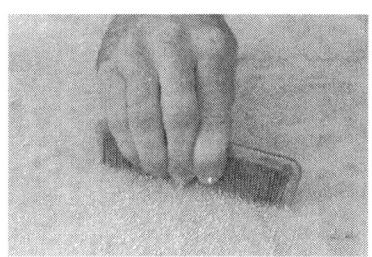

A standard hair comb can also put a surfable texture to existing wax on a board. Nowadays, "wax combs" are a standard of surfing preparation.

The first surf leashes were little more than a doggie collar and a bunji cord. These days they are a mandatory ingredient of surfing preparation and safety.

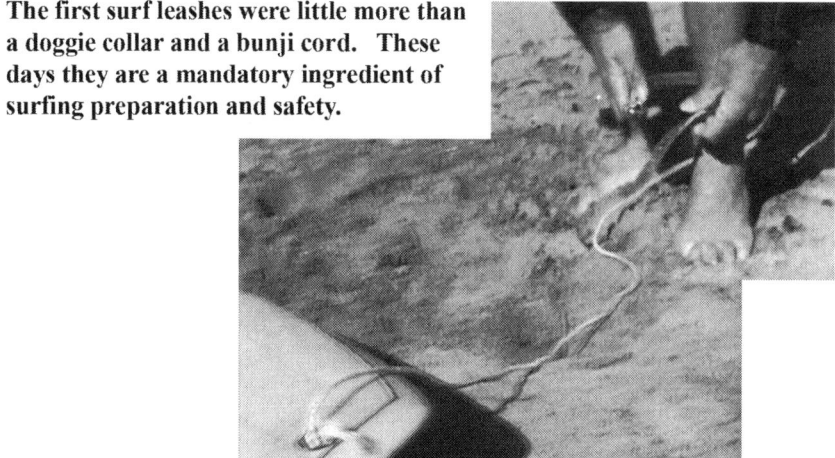

Beach Preparation

between sets of waves and riding surfers. Reef breaks are usually the easiest to paddle out to, in that they usually break in one pronounced peak, and the surfer need only to paddle to either side of it. One disadvantage might be that, although it is an easy paddle, it could also be a long paddle, in that some reefs break as far out as a quarter mile in the ocean. After these minor preparations, considerations and evaluations, it is time to enter the water.

PADDLING THROUGH SURF

Paddling a surfboard is the first step toward going anywhere in surfing. The basics of paddling through surf and around surfers should be mastered until they come without thinking. To begin with, set the board in the water and lie on top of it. Try adjusting your position forward. Too far forward and the board will nose under as you paddle. Too far back, and the board will paddle too slow. The trick is to find the position where the board paddles the fastest and the nose breaks just barely above the surface of the water.

Prone paddling is lying down and "swimming" your board out to the surf, paddling arm over arm. Knee paddling, which is most effective only on longer boards, is done by stroking with arms together, much like rowing a rowboat. To turn the board to the right, paddle harder with the left hand, and vice-versa, to turn to the left. To turn sharper or pivot turn, drag or paddle backwards with the arm in the direction in which you wish to turn, and forward with the other. Your arms will be paddling in opposite directions, and your board will pivot in a turn. The same works when sitting on a surfboard. To turn, move slightly to the rear of the board and swivel your feet under the water. The board will pivot around in the opposite direction.

Getting through a small surf of one to two feet is usually no problem. The surfer just keeps paddling through the wave or white water with little resistance. On larger waves, this gets a little rougher. Paddling through three to four foot waves can be most easily done by sliding forward just before the wave hits. This will sink the nose of the board below the impact of the white water and give the surfer stability under the turbulence. Hang on tight till the wave passes over, and you will surface on the other side.

PADDLING THRU SURF

PRONE PADDLE — arm over arm, as in swimming

KNEE PADDLING — arms together, like rowing a boat.

THRU SMALL BREAKING WAVE
Grab nose of board
Put head down.
Lean forward, sink nose of board.

Come up outside of break.

THRU LARGE BREAKING WAVE
Roll over, underneath board.
Grab nose of board,
TIGHTLY
Pull nose under water.
Wait for break to pass over.
Surface outside of break.

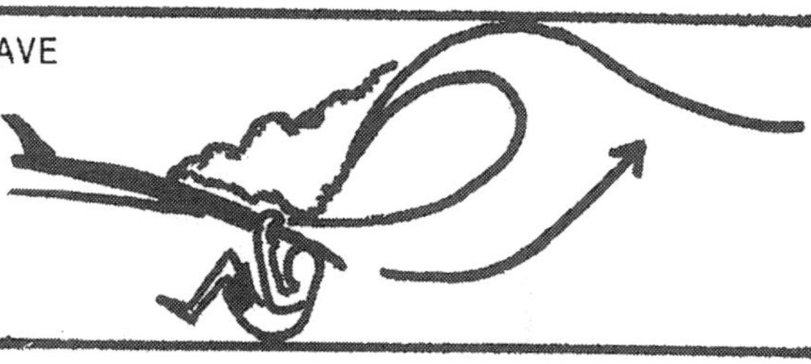

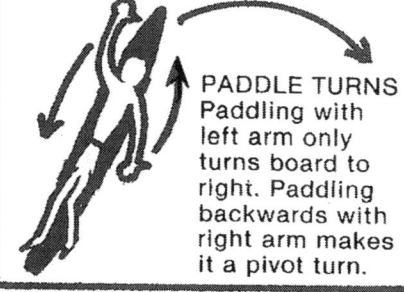

PADDLE TURNS Paddling with left arm only turns board to right. Paddling backwards with right arm makes it a pivot turn.

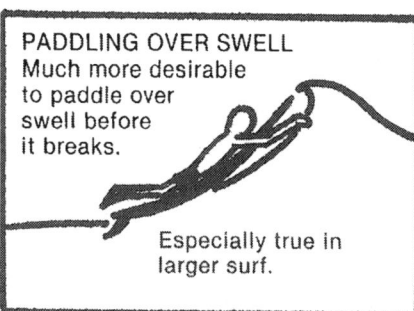

PADDLING OVER SWELL
Much more desirable to paddle over swell before it breaks.

Especially true in larger surf.

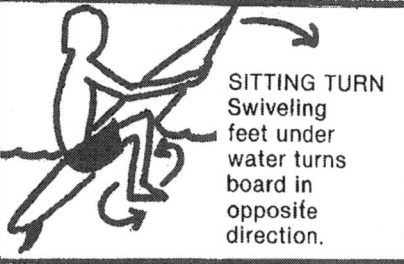

SITTING TURN Swiveling feet under water turns board in opposite direction.

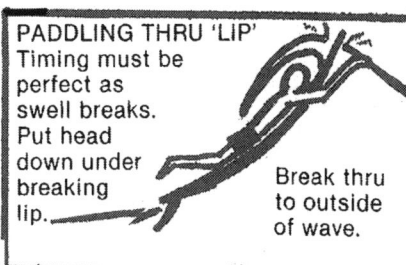

PADDLING THRU 'LIP'
Timing must be perfect as swell breaks. Put head down under breaking lip.

Break thru to outside of wave.

Paddling thru Surf

The technique changes for paddling through larger and more powerful waves. As a surfer approaches a four to eight foot breaking whitewater wave, he rolls over with his board skeg up, grabs as tightly as he can onto the nose and pulls it and himself under the water as the wave hits. The primary rule is to hang on tight when the wave bucks, pulls, tosses and turns you under the turbulence. Some surfers have been known to hang on with hands, legs, feet, teeth and all their might when a big one hits. Eventually you will either surface on the other side of the wave or end up on the beach as it hits the shore. The former is more desirable.

If paddling through an eight foot wave can get difficult, then in still larger surf it can be almost impossible, depending on how long and hard one can hang on. For this reason, it can be most desirable to get through larger waves before they break. This may take some timing and some fast paddling, but it is well worth the effort. The effort is to get through a larger wave before it is a large *breaking* wave. This can still be accomplished up till the last instant of the break by bursting through the lip as the wave breaks. As the steepening swell approaches, one must paddle fast and hard to get over the wave before it breaks on him. The last instant the surfer is paddling up the swell and the lip of water is breaking down. The surfer must duck his head under the breaking lip and burst through the sheet of water out to the other side to open water.

In most cases, the surfer can then relax. However, there is a situation called "getting sucked back over the falls." This happens when the surfer has been too slow or too late in his paddling, and ends up going back over with the breaking lip, instead of through it. This can be a most unpleasant sensation in surfing, usually resulting in loss of surfboard and self-esteem. To avoid this type of occurrence, practice paddling techniques and wave judgment at many smaller and easier surfing locations before tackling more difficult situations.

TRAFFIC IN THE SURF

Traffic in the surf is about as important as traffic on the street, and a lot of times as dangerous. One must learn to deal with it in order to survive. Paddling out through no-surf conditions is easy. One need only pick a direction, and paddle that way without bumping into anybody. But it is when you see those medium to large swells on the horizon, that things start to get scary. All of a sudden everything changes. Surfers start paddling in all directions, waves are breaking where you don't expect them, loose surfboards are hurtling around in the water and air, and persons on surfboards are coming at you from all directions at speeds of up to 20 miles per hour.

What does one do? First of all, try to be outside the surfing line-up when the swells start breaking. But if you are caught inside, start paddling for the shoulder of the waves; the smallest part of the wave the farthest from the break. Most good surfers will be riding close to the break or curl, and the shoulder will be the safest route. If you are too far from the shoulder, or the surfer riding the wave is in a collision course with the shoulder route, then the paddler should wait for the surfer to ride by, then paddle through the lip or break behind the riding surfer. When in doubt, go behind the riding surfer. Dealing with the break of a wave is always easier than dealing with a 20 mile per hour surfboard accompanied by an irate surfer.

Even on a crowded wave, with five or more surfers riding, the best choice is either an early route over the shoulder or a late route through the break. Either way, avoid the crowd. However, there are those occasions when you are so close to the wave that there doesn't seem to be time for all of the surfers to go by before collision occurs. At a time like this, one must pick a gap in the crowd of riders and 'go for it.' This can be one of the most exciting experiences in surfing. Not only does the paddler get an excellent super close-up view of surfers in action, but he gets enough panic in the process to drive him through to safety over the top of the wave.

Most of the time a surfer won't run over a paddler if he can avoid it (without inconveniencing himself). The best rule for paddlers is to stay out of the way. If you can't get out of the way, and you find yourself in collision course with one of these surfers with a maniacal look in his eye, then roll over at the last second, hang on to the nose of your board and pull it and yourself under water. Not only will your board become a shield against the on-coming surfer, but if you do it right, your fin will also cut half-way through his board as he runs over you. This may somewhat avenge your feelings of helplessness at being run over. One must then refer to courses on self-defense for handling the ensuing situation.

TRAFFIC IN THE SURF

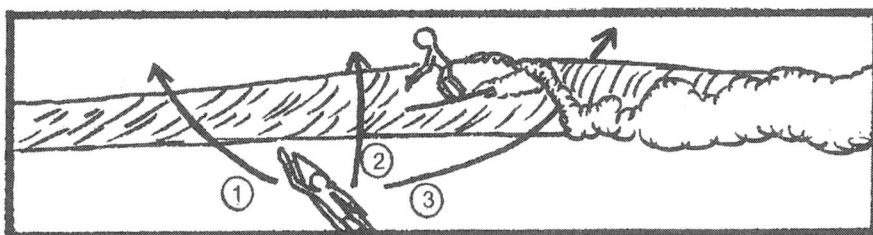

PADDLING THRU SURF LINE UP — 1. Best choice, over shoulder of wave. 2. Bad choice, collision. 3. 2nd. best choice, wait for surfer to go by, then go thru lip or white water.

THRU CROWDED CONDITIONS — 1. Best choice, but too late for that now. 2. Scary choice, possible collision. 3. Only choice left now, wait for crowd to go by, then go thru lip.

UNAVOIDABLE COLLISION — Usually caused by surfer who doesn't care if he misses you. Roll over at last second, pull nose of board underwater and use board as shield.

LOG JAM IN WHITE WATER — Unpredictable chaos, take no chances getting hit by bouncing board. Roll over, pull nose of board underwater and use board as shield.

Traffic in the Surf

Occasionally, a surfer paddling out will find that all the surfers riding in his path are wiped out by a close-out wave and a series of accidental falls. The paddler then finds himself faced with a churning mass of white-water, seeded indiscriminately with loose, bouncing, spearing surfboards. This is like being downstream at a logging pond when the dam breaks. As these boards come bounding your way, "roll over, grab the nose of your board," pull down as deep as you can, use your board for a shield and listen for the thunks and thuds. This is not the favorite situation in the sport of surfing. However, all these situations can be handled safely. Just use the same amount of caution you do when crossing the freeway at rush hour on roller skates. And enjoy yourself.

WAVE DIRECTIONS AND SURFER'S STANCES

Now that you have been surfing for a while, you might like to know which way you were surfing and how you were standing. Were you going left, right, across the face, or hopping the shoulder? Are you regular foot, goofy foot or standing parallel? Wave directions are determined from the surfer's vantage point as he takes off. If he goes to his right, it is a right wave; to his left, a left. Point breaks usually break in long right lines. Beach breaks usually have both rights and lefts, with the really quality waves being to the left (especially at most California beaches). A reef break will usually break in a peak with a right off one side and a left off the other. Some peaks have equally good lefts and rights, but most favor one direction of break.

A curl is the breaking section of wave; the face of the wave is the steep unbroken section of the swell; a line-up is a long section of the face in the direction of the surfer's ride (as in "a long right line-up"). A shoulder is the less steep part of the face toward the end of the line-up or at the edges of a peak. A section is a part of wave breaking in front of the surfer and the even curling of the wave. A section that breaks all down the face of a wave makes it a close-out, and an all white-water wave. A tube is the hollow part of a wave formed by the curl as it throws out in front of the face of the wave as it breaks.

WAVE DIRECTIONS
AND SURFER'S STANCES

RIGHT BREAK WAVE — Determined from surfer's position.

LEFT BREAK WAVE — Surfer riding backside.

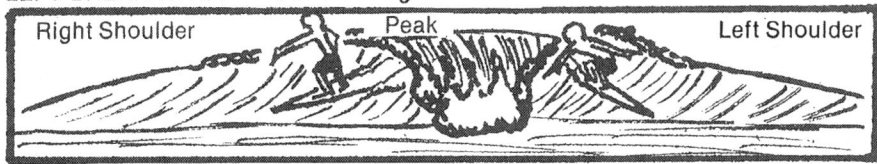

PEAK BREAK WAVE — With right and left line up.

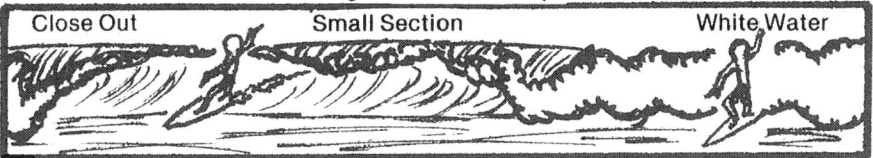

CLOSE OUT WAVE — With surfers straightening out and in soup.

RIGHT TUBE — with shoulder.

LEFT TUBE — with line up.

REGULAR FOOT — rides facing a right breaking wave.

REGULAR FOOT — rides 'back side' on left break wave.

GOOFY FOOT — rides 'back side' on right break wave.

GOOFY FOOT — Rides facing a left break wave.

Wave Directions and Surfer's Stances

Surfers usually stand with one foot markedly in front of the other. This is like being right handed or left handed. A regular foot is the right handed way of surfing. A regular foot surfs with most of his weight on his right foot, which is his trailing foot, and uses his right leg for turning and wave positioning. He stands *left foot forward* and faces a right break wave. On a left break wave, a regular foot surfs "backside" with his back to the wave.

A "goofy foot" is the left handed way of surfing. He surfs *right* foot forward and faces left breaking waves. Most of his balance and turning is done with his trailing left foot. Most surfers are at an advantage riding while facing a wave. Therefore, a regular foot seems to have an advantage in right break waves, and a goofy foot an advantage in left break waves. Backside is a regular foot going left, or a goofy foot going right. Going backside requires a slightly different technique that is usually considered a little more difficult.

Now that you are completely confused about what is going on, this might be a little simpler: If you are a regular foot you will probably be more comfortable riding right breaks. If you are a goofy foot, you will be more at home on lefts.

RIDING THE WHITEWATER

Riding the whitewater is a very important phase for the very beginning surfer. It gives you your first experience at actually riding your surfboard. Riding whitewater can be the first introduction to forward motion, balance, trim and the feel of your board for flotation and stability. Every wave has white water after the initial break of the wave or swell. The best beaches for this are where the whitewater rolls for a long way after the wave has broken. Crashing tubes and shorebreaks where the waves break right on the beach should be avoided. The surfer should also allow a few seconds between the initial break of the wave and the point where he picks it up.

Catching the whitewater is very easy. You merely lie on your board pointed toward the beach and let the white water overtake you and propel you toward the beach. Sometimes a few paddling strokes will insure that the wave picks you up. If you are too close to the break of the wave you may experience an unpleasant cracking in your back as the tube splits your waist with its initial break.

RIDING WHITEWATER

WAVE BREAKS OUTSIDE while surfer waits for wall of whitewater.

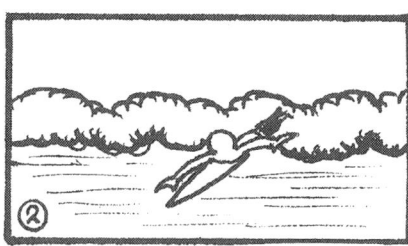

A FEW PADDLE STROKES insure that surfer catches the whitewater.

IF BOARD NOSES UNDER, surfer moves back. If board slows, surfer moves forward.

SURFER TURNS BOARD with pressure on rail in direction of the turn.

SURFER STANDS from 'push up' position by pulling feet under him to center of board.

SURFER MOVES FORWARD if tail sinks, surfer moves back if board noses under.

TURNS ARE MADE with very gradual pressure in the direction of the turn.

PULLOUT IS MADE by sinking tail of board and grabbing onto nose.

Riding Whitewater

This may be followed by a lifting and then a sinking sensation as the wave swallows you up and takes your board from you in your first wipe out. Moral: do not let the wave break on you.

Once the wave is propelling you forward, you can start to get the feel of surfing. If you nose under, you are too far forward: move back. If you start to lose the whitewater, you are too far back: move foreward. You may also notice that you are angling slightly to the left or the right. This is not bad, but merely your first (maybe involuntary) turning of your board with pressure to one side or the other of the board. You can learn to control the turning by applying pressure to the direction to which you wish to turn.

Now, as you start to feel comfortable with your forward motion and your board, start to stand. This is done by lifting yourself up with your arms in a "push up" position and pulling your feet underneath you. Put your feet in the center of the board (not toward either rail) and with one foot, (probably your left) very much in front of the other in a semi-wide stance (feet two feet apart). If you start to nose under, move or lean back. If you start to slow down, move or lean forward. Stand directly above the center of your board, or you will tip over to the left or right. As you get the feel of it, you can angle to the left or right by leaning slightly in the direction you wish to go, with weight primarily on the trailing foot.

With practice you will find that the sooner you stand up and the faster your board is going, the easier it will be to get to your feet and control your board. These early techniques can go a long way toward familiarizing you with surfing and your board. Catch a lot of waves and ride as long as you can on each one. And as soon as you get comfortable with yourself in the "Soup," move on to catching swell and riding waves.

CATCHING A WAVE

Here comes your first try at actual surfing. Assuming that you have conquered the challenge of beach preparation, paddling through the surf and traffic in the surf. You are now out in the ocean with unsaid number of surfers waiting for a wave for your first attempt at riding. See if you can find a wave to yourself. Common surf courtesy dictates that the first person riding a wave and closest to the break, has wave possession. Don't take off in front of somebody who is already riding. In crowded conditions, this may also be saying, "Don't take off at all," because there will seem to be somebody on every wave. Either find a smaller inside wave with nobody on it or take off with other beginning surfers who won't need to be quite so possessive of the entire wave.

Catching a Wave . . .

It helps to start off in small waves.

Paddle furiously till you feel the surge of the wave pushing you.

Arch your back and lean back to keep from "pearling" (nosing under).

Lift your body by doing a "push up" on the board and pull your feet under you to a middle balance point on the board.

Stand and get your balance. Move or lean forward on the board if you slow down or start to lose wave. Lean back if you start to "Pearl". Positioning your feet left or right will cause the board to turn left or right.

Ride in trimmed position on your board (somewhere in the middle) so that board glides easily across the swell and whitewater.

Turn to the left or right away from the whitewater towards the open water on the face of the swell.

From "The Living Curl", Marty Sugarman, Doheny's "Boneyards".

Catching a Wave

Anyway, here it comes, your first wave. Nobody around and it is all yours. You're sitting on your board watching the approaching swell getting larger and steeper each second. As the swell gets closer to you, swivel your feet underwater to turn your board around heading in the same direction as the swell is traveling, usually straight at the beach. Time your paddling so that you will be right on the swell just before it starts to break. Paddle hard as the swell lifts the tail of your board. The swell will start to carry you down the face of the wave. At this point arch your back to keep the board from nosing under the wave.

Now your board should be planing across the wave, preferably at an angle away from the break of the wave. So stand up! This is done by grabbing the rails of your board (edges), lifting yourself up and putting your feet under you. Now you are surfing. Start to get the feel of your board. If you are too far forward, the board will start to nose under. If you are too far back, you will lose speed and start to float out over the top of the wave. The perfect position for a beginning ride is somewhere in the middle of your board where you are planing across the face of the wave at an even speed. This is called trimming.

You should be trimming at an angle to the wave so that you are constantly riding on the swell and face of the wave with the break of the wave behind you. This is called "shooting the curl" (as you will remember from your first Gidget movie). The trick is to keep riding across the wave in this manner until the wave breaks in front of you (closes out) or dissipates under you (dies out). If the wave closes out, then straighten out in front of the white water and ride toward the beach. If it dies out, then paddle back out to the line up.

Either way, "Congratulations." You are now a surfer. Don't be discouraged because you fell off, tipped over, nosed under, lost your board, or were afraid to take off in the first place. You now know the basics and you are on your way. Get back out there and try your next wave. Look around and study the surfers around you who are getting good rides. Watch their timing, paddling and wave positioning as they drop into waves. Soon you will be a top surfer just like they are, for nobody admits to being a beginner for more than about the first fifteen minutes of his surfing career.

Now you are ready to really get into it.

BEGINNING RIDES

Beginning rides in surfing should be primarily to get the feel of your surfboard, your ability and the waves you are riding. Even the most experienced surfers go through a short period of "beginning rides" almost every time they go out in the water, just to get 'tuned up' or get a location 'wired.' Once you have caught the wave, you should make an easy turn to the right (assuming that you are a regular foot on a right wave). This turn is made by resting most of your weight on your right foot (trailing foot) and almost 'swinging' your board underneath you to the right. This done in much the same manner as a baseball player swings a bat, only using your legs and board.

At this stage in surfing, you are not really banking your board into turns or using body weight placement to gain speed, but merely swinging the board in the direction in which you wish to go. With the board turned in the wave direction, you should begin to trim it up. This is done by shifting and shuffling your weight forward and backward for the maximum speed across the face of the wave. Normally, the further forward you get, the faster you will go. But sometimes on a slower wave, you will 'mush out' to a stop if you are too far forward. When this happens, shuffle back and you will actually gain a better trim.

As you experiment with various stages of trim across the face of the wave, you will occasionally find that sections of wave will break in front of you on the wave. When this happens, shuffle back a little bit and angle your board down to the bottom of the wave and ride under white water formed by the section until once again you are on the open face of the wave.

Many times you will find that immediately following a section of breaking wave is a shoulder or slower part to a wave. When you come to a shoulder, you will probably have to alter your board direction a little to stay in the wave. This is a cut back or turn back maneuver. It is done the same way as a turn, by 'swinging' the board around, but this time to your left, to keep you in the swell action of the shoulder. A cut back may be done easier if you shift your right foot toward the left rail of the tail of your board and put pressure on this foot. This will put some drive into the swinging turn of your maneuver. Either way, you should now be heading more in the direction of the beach, moving *with* the swell rather than across it.

Beginning Rides

As you watch the swell to your right, you may find that it begins to line up again in front of you, and it is time again to start trimming across the face. Once again you must make a right turn to come out of the direction taken by the cut back. This turn may be done by placing your right foot toward the right rail of the tail of your board, and putting pressure on it. This pressure will put some drive into the other swinging action of your turn. You may find that you come out of this turn with more speed than your other turn by swinging alone. You are once again in a position to retain your various degrees of trim to suit the break across the face of the wave.

As you watch the wave while you are trimming, you may spot a section of break that is either too long or too powerful for you to ride under. As this section 'closes out' the wave in front of you, you may want to exit the wave to avoid the close out. This is done by pulling out over the top of the wave. A pull out is a turning maneuver out over the top of the wave. Once again, place your right foot toward the rail of the tail of your board and put pressure on that foot. As you should have some speed from trimming, this pressure should be sufficient to drive and angle you out over the top of the wave. A little swinging action would snap you out with style, and the wave will close out with you safely out the back.

If you are too late for a pull out, or wish to ride all the way to the shore, you can ride in the white water. This is done by simply angling your board to the bottom of the wave with a turn back maneuver as the wave closes out. You can then vary the angle of your board in the white water from extreme angle to straight toward the beach. In this manner you can ride all the way to the shore and step off on the sand if the conditions are right.

You may also find yourself in conditions for riding some good backside waves. Should this occur, you will find that your initial turn will be like that of turn back on a frontside wave. You will place your right foot toward the left rail of the tail of your board and put pressure to swing the board to the left and put yourself in the direction of trim. Should you come to a shoulder on a backside wave, you will find that your turn-back into the swell will be like that of a standard right turn on a right wave. Pressure to the right will swing you back into the wave or swell, and pressure to the left will put you in a trim direction.

Aside from these basic differences, surfing a left or backside wave is done in the same manner as a right breaking wave. However, you will find that 'backside' has an entirely different feel to it, and that it requires a slight modification in that you may not be able to trim quite as directly across the face of the backside wave.

Beginning Rides . . .

TAKE OFF - Arch back to keep from "pearling" after you feel you've caught wave.

TURN - or angle away from white water across swell of wave.

WHITE WATER SECTION - May break on you. Keep Surfing!

STEEP SECTION - may cause you to move to tailblock to keep from "pearling".

TURN BACK - with foot pressure on left rail of tail while twisting body.

TURN - with foot pressure on right rail of tail while leaning towards wave

KICK-OUT - by sinking tail and swinging board out of wave.

CAUTION - Late take-off may lead to Pearl Diving!

Marty Sugarman at Doheny's "Bone Yard", from Jamie Budge's "The Living Curl". flopped to look more like Miki Dora.

Beginning Rides

From these techniques in beginning surfing you should be able to do quite a bit of surfing in many varied wave conditions. As you get the feel of different waves and your own ability to handle them, you will soon find yourself executing sharper turns, quicker trimming and a whole repertoire of more difficult maneuvers to be explained in later chapters.

RULES OF THE ROAD

Now that you are out there surfing and handling yourself like one of the crowd, let me explain some of the things that are going to be expected of you by your fellow surfers. First of all, every surfer is very possessive of 'his' wave. He may even be possessive of it if it isn't *his* wave. But the official wave possession goes to the surfer who is first into the wave and closest to the breaking curl. If you start to take off in his way, he will probably yell bloody murder at you. This doesn't mean you can't take off. It just tells you where you stand if you do.

If the surfer in the curl should wipe out or get stuck in the whitewater behind an un-makeable section, then once again it is open wave to whoever can get into the wave and establish possession next to the curl. The surfer on the wave has certain manners required of himself, primarily not to run anybody over. In almost any wave situation, the surfer will have the time and room to cut back or slow down enough to let any paddler get over the wave. Sometimes a surfer may find himself weaving through the crowd of paddlers going every which way he can to find an open route. And sometimes a surfer can't find an open route. Then it comes back on the paddler to stay out of the way of the surfer.

When a surfer is tucked into a hot curl or driving at full speed to beat a possible close out, he isn't about to slow down for you and let himself get gobbled by a gnarley tube. So keep an eye out for those tight situations and make sure that you can stay clear of them. Getting your hair wet paddling through a little soup isn't going to hurt as much as having your board sliced in two by a razor sharp fin of a speeding surfer.

ADVICE ON WIPE-OUTS

And watch your own wipeouts. You are bound to have some and most of them can be calculated. Don't try any risky maneuvers unless the path is clear. Should you find yourself wiping out, then land yourself to the wave-ward side of your board. That way your board won't run you over the second after you wipe out. The water is also deeper in the wave than in front of it, so you can avoid hitting the bottom. In a larger wave, you should swim hard to get

RULES OF THE ROAD

WAVE POSSESSION — goes to surfer first in the wave and closest to curl.

UN-MAKEABLE SECTION — gives wave possession to new surfer closest to curl.

TURNING BACK FOR PADDLERS — is a responsibility of surfer to avoid collision.

MAKING WAY FOR SURFERS — in tight positions is responsibility of paddlers.

DIVE INTO WAVE — if you wipe out, the water is deeper and there are no rocks.

IF YOU LOSE YOUR BOARD — stay under water long enough for it to come down.

DON'T LOSE BOARD IN CROWD — Hang on to it and drag feet till you come to a stop.

LOOK FOR ROCK BOILS — which show rocks under surface. Ride high over danger.

through the wave and not come back over the falls, which would probably leave you bounding around in the white water with your loose board.

Second point, if you do lose your board, stay under water long enough for it to come down, should it be hurtling around in the air. Too many surfers have come up looking for their board only to have it come down on their head. If you think this is a possibility, stay down with your arms over your head.

If you are trying, you should be able to avoid losing your board; and you should be trying if there are other surfers paddling out. If you start to wipe out in a crowd, let yourself fall carefully on your board and prone ride around surfers and out of danger. If you're in a dead collision course, you can fall on your board, grab the rails and drag your feet and probably come to a standstill while the danger and wave passes by. Whatever the circumstances, do all you can to avoid collision with other surfers, paddlers, swimmers, seals and whatever.

Also on the collision course can be submerged reefs and large rocks. These reveal themselves to be just under the surface when there are circular 'rock boils' or ripples on top of shallow water. Avoid surfing over these rock boils, as you may come to a dead stop when your skeg catches a rock and you hurl onto the reef. If you are riding a wave and these menaces appear, ride high in the wave to float over the danger.

Other menaces high on the list include drainpipes, buoy lines and sunken pilings. And of course, kelp, which can bring even the most experienced surfer's ride to an abrupt halt when his fin catches. All one can really safely do is ride around or over, high in the wave.

And now you know the situations you shouldn't get into and what to do when you do get into them. Be advised of the rules of the road for tolerable relations with fellow wave hogs, and watch yourself and fellow surfers in wipeout situations.

HAZARDS OF THE SURF

For the most part, the hazards of surfing are quite minimal. The dangers are usually more interesting than they are actually dangerous. However, there are conditions and hazards which should be watched for and treated with respect.

Hazards of the Surf

BIG SURF would be one condition that can change a normally pleasant experience into a dangerous struggle. The struggle is in paddling through consistent pounding surf with currents sweeping you down the back and into other hazards such as jetties and piers. The best way for a novice to handle really big surf is to watch it from the beach. If you want to give it a try, find a familiar location with surf that you know from past experience.

RIP TIDES are a result of surf washing up on the beach and flowing back out to sea in rivers or currents. These rip tides can carry you miles out to sea in extreme cases. If you find yourself in a rip tide, paddle or swim to the side of it and let the breaking surf carry you into the shore. This may call for a lot of holding your breath and dunking under waves, but it is safer than ending up in the middle of the ocean.

ROCKS, JETTIES & PIERS can be havoc in large surf when the currents of the waves may pull you into these hazards. Understand the currents and line-up of the surf before you get into a situation where these may endanger you. When in doubt, stay clear. **CORAL & ROCKS** just under the surface of the water can cause deep cuts and bruises. If you are surfing in shallow water, be extremely careful where you fall. Don't risk any wipeouts.

CUTS ON SEA URCHINS OR CORAL should be watched for infection. Remove all broken parts of coral or urchin from the cut and clean thoroughly with disinfectant. **JELLYFISH & MAN-OF-WAR JELLFISH** can cause painful and burning stings with their long tentacles. These are usually more uncomfortable than dangerous. Cleanse thoroughly and use vinegar to alleviate pain. Should you be extremely uncomfortable from a sting from a large Man of War, treat for shock and get to a doctor.

SHARKS can be deadly. The best way to handle sharks is to leave immediately, calmly and slowly. Don't thrash, panic, or struggle. This will arouse his animal instincts. Should a shark be in an encounter course with you, the best deterrant is a kick on the nose. Do not enter shark areas with any cuts or bleeding as this will attract sharks. Although many sharks may be more curious than hungry, the communication gap between sharks and surfers is extremely unpredictable. Leave the water at any sign of sharks.

SURFERS however are their own biggest hazards, causing more accidents with their own collisions than any other menace. Observe Rules of the Road, as explained earlier, and surf as if the other surfer is a little crazy. He probably is.

ASK AROUND before entering strange waters. Surf spots have a way of producing their own unique hazards. One may have railroad spikes just under the surface, and another piranhas. Find out what you are getting into before you are into it.

HAZARDS OF THE SURF

BIG SURF can tumble, toss and exhaust you. Beware of strong forces at work.

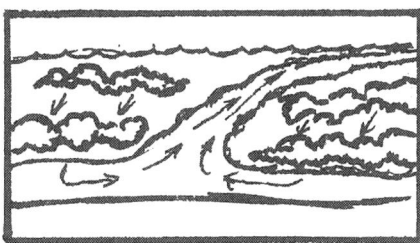

RIP TIDES can carry you out to sea. Swim clear of these rivers in the ocean.

ROCKS IN THE SURF can cause currents that will sweep you into them. Keep clear!

CORAL under the water can cause deep cuts and infection. Watch where you step.

SEA URCHIN (and coral) PARTS should be removed from cuts before thoroughly cleaning.

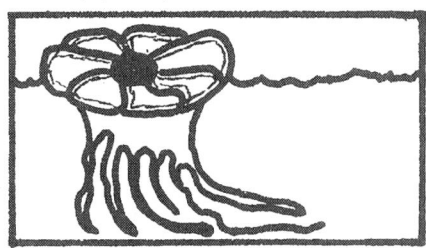

JELLYFISH & MEN OF WAR can sting. Clean wound, soak in vinegar, or rub with sand.

SHARKS can be deadly. Leave water slowly and calmy if you encounter sharks.

BIGGEST MENACE OF ALL are surfers out of control. Stay clear of these hazards.

NOTE: Check with local surfers for information about any hazard that may exist at a particular location.

Hazards in the Surf...

BIG SURF - can tumble, toss and exhaust you. Beward of strong forces at work.
RIP TIDES - can carry you out to sea. Stay clear of these rivers in the ocean.

WIPEOUTS - can dump you on rock piles, jetties, piers and other surfers.

Rocks, reefs and other obstacles can pop out of the water.

BIGGEST HAZARD OF ALL -

OTHER SURFERS may not always welcome you in "their" surf.

They can push, kick-out and run you over.

Images from Jamie Budge's "The Living Curl" and "The Californians".

SURFING THEORY

Surfing theory can be explained by anything from "you ride a wave because it's fun" to the most complex principles of aerodynamics involving lift, drag, turning radius and planing surfaces. My own description will be rather brief, as the object of this book is not to discuss and prove the different theoretical approaches involved, but to explain what is actually available to the novice surfer. But for a brief example of how surfing works, here is an analogy.

A surfer is much like the pilot of a small airplane. His surfboard is his flying machine and the waves are his currents of air across which he flies. Every maneuver that a surfer makes is his form of flying across the face of the wave for maximum speed, position and advantage for a better ride. His turns, turn-backs, trimming and other maneuvers are all executed by the hydrodynamic relationship of the planing surface of the board to currents of the wave that he rides. Turning is a result of "for every action there is an equal and opposite reaction" combined with the hydro-foil effect of the edge (rail) of the board on the face of the wave. Trimming and stalling are both examples of surface area drag and reduced drag of the planing area of the board across the surface of the wave. Nose riding and side-slipping are examples of how these surface areas can be directed with forward and aft weight positioning.

Because of this hydrodynamic interplay between surfboard and wave, much care is given by experienced surfers to the choice of waves they ride and the type of surfboard on which they ride these waves. The more desirable wave to the experienced surfer is one considered faster and hollower. Because of the rapid flow of water created by this type of wave, all the aero-dynamics involved are increased in their effectiveness. The surfer experiences a greater potential for maneuvering, along with a greater possibility for wave area on which to execute these maneuvers.

Because of this potential for greater freedom and speed on a wave, the surfer will choose a board that is the best hydrodynamic combination between his weight and style of surfing and the waves he will ride. Thus, the evolving theories of surfboard design are all aimed at a greater freedom for the surfer, made possible by the accelerated turning, trimming and wave positioning resulting from the advanced planing surfaces of the modern surfboard.

Surfing Theory

In other words, "with a hot stick on a hollow tube, you can get a stoking good ride." If you keep this in mind you will be well on the road to the top surfing pursued by the most experienced professionals in the sport today. And although a little theory may help you to know what is going on underneath you as you surf, the proof is in the pudding and the surfing is out in the water. The next pages are designed to get you started experiencing the greater sensations in the maneuvers of surfing.

The aerodynamics of flight are somewhat similar to the hydrodynamics of surfing as you "fly" across the face of the wave.

Climb . . .

Drop . . .

Bank into Turn . . .

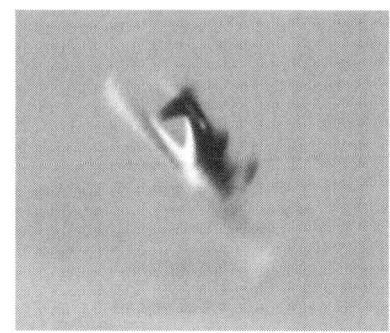
Spin Out of Control . . .

INTRODUCTION TO MANEUVERING

To the beginning surfer, the following pages about maneuvering may seem a bit complex. This is not aimed at confusing the novice even though it may seem so. As a surfer advances, he will find all these descriptions relevant to better maneuvering. In the meantime, look at the illustrations and read the brief descriptions below:

TURNING MANEUVERS
Bottom Turn — to turn in wave direction and to gain speed by leaning and banking off bottom of wave.
Top Turn — to turn in wave direction and to gain speed by leaning and banking off top of wave.
Turn Back — to turn back as wave slows down by banking and leaning around toward break of wave.
"S" Maneuver — combination of turn back and bottom turn for positioning at shoulder of wave.
Climbing and Dropping — combination of bottom turn and turn back for turning up and down across face of wave for speed.
Kick Out — turning maneuver out over top of wave to exit and end ride.
Roller Coaster — a kick out that ends by coming back over with break of wave.

TRIMMING MANEUVERS
Trimming — to gain speed and set straight course across face of wave by moving forward and back on board.
Stalling — to trim surfboard to go slow across face of wave by moving toward tail of board.
Nose Riding — to trim surfboard on very nose of board for maximum speed and effect by moving all the way forward on board.
Side Slipping — to move sideways down face of wave by releasing fin from face of wave.
Curl Rides — to ride completely inside curl or tube of wave by slowing board while wave breaks over.
Back Side — to ride with back to wave while riding and performing all the above maneuvers.

These are the maneuvers that give surfers every thrill there is in the sport of surfing. It is by perfecting these methods of turning and trimming that a surfer gains mastery over the waves he rides. In beginning surfing, the novice will find the impulse to do these maneuvers merely from surfing and examing the waves he rides. From the impulse to do a maneuver comes the attempt. And from the attempts come perfection. The more detailed descriptions on the following pages will further you in that pursuit.

BOTTOM TURNS & TOP TURNS

The bottom turn is the most basic of all surfing maneuvers. It is usually the first maneuver that a surfer does on a wave. The turn gives the surfer his initial speed in establishing trim across the face of the wave, as well as establishing his initial direction. Setting up for the bottom turn begins when the surfer first drops into his wave. With feet at somewhat of a wide stance to avoid nosing under, the surfer drives his board down to the bottom of his wave.

As he approaches the bottom of the wave, he may actually shoot out in front of the slope of the wave before beginning his turn. At this point he begins to lean to the right while putting pressure on his right foot. This will swing the board around in the proper direction as the pressure on the tail will sink it deep into the face of the wave. With proper banking, this will cause the boar to being to carve up the face of the wave while it gains acceleration.

As the surfer comes out of his bottom turn he must begin to lean and move his weight forward to maintain the speed established by the turn. Because the turn establishes wave direction, with proper timing the surfer can come out of his turn and place himself in perfect trim without any loss of speed. Although in the description above, there is specific reference to pressure here and leaning there, etc., every surfer must develop his coordination of these efforts.

Each maneuver in surfing is the expression of each rider's individuality, and therefore one surfer might turn mostly with the pressure in his knees and feet, while another might gain all his turning with twisting of the shoulders and banking into the turn. Individual styles can be studied and somewhat emulated by novices wishing to study the effects of one particular approach to a maneuver. With experience, each surfer will discover his own combination of banking, leaning, placing pressure and torqueing for best results with each maneuver. The specific illustrations and written references in this book should only be used as a buie for each surfer's experimentation and practice.

The top turn is begun with the surfer angling across the top of the wave just before it breaks. While the surfer angles to the left, he waits for the wave to develop in steepness. At a point just before he reaches the break of the wave, the surfer swings his board around primarily with pressure and pivoting in the knees. As the board swings around, the surfer's body direction changes with it so that both surfer and board are traveling away from the break of wave. At this time, the surfer should begin moving forward for establishing trim across the top of the wave.

BOTTOM TURNS
& TOP TURNS

BOTTOM TURN begins with surfer driving board down face of wave.

AT BOTTOM of wave, surfer begins to swing board in direction of turn.

GAINING SPEED from turn, surfer banks board and carves across wave.

COMING OUT OF TURN surfer moves forward on board to retain speed.

TOP TURN begins with surfer angling across top of wave.

AS WAVE STEEPENS surfer banks board around with action in his knees.

BOARD SWINGS AROUND in correct wave direction away from break.

SURFER COMES OUT OF TURN high in top of wave and begins to trim.

Bottom Turns, Top Turns ...

Johnny Fain, one of the original Malibu "Hot Doggers", demonstrates a perfect longboard BOTTOM TURN.

Works on Short Boards too. David Nuuhiwa carves a hard BOTTOM TURN on a Hollywood-by-the-Sea left.

Midget Farrelly whips a longboard, change-of-direction, go-left, go-right TOP TURN.

From Jamie Budge's "The Living Curl" and "The Californians"

Top Turns

The top turn is used mostly when the surfer wants to gain speed and position from turning without dropping to the bottom of the wave. This can be most useful on slower waves where a better trim may be established. With proper execution of these two maneuvers, the surfer will have distinct advantage in beginning his ride.

TURN BACK & "S" MANEUVER

The turn back is the other half of the pair of turning maneuvers that give the surfer complete control of his position on the face of the wave. A turn back combined with a bottom turn (or forward turn) makes for a complete "S" maneuver that takes the surfer from the top of a shouldering wave down to the bottom of the wave and back up again. A series of bottom turns and turn backs can result in the surfer climbing and dropping across the wave gaining speed with each maneuver. For this reason the interplay of turning and turning back are of essential importance to effective surfing.

The surfer should begin his turn-back as he reaches the shoulder of the wave. At this point, the break of the wave has slowed down and the line up is no longer building up in front of him. The surfer turns back to allow time for the line-up to form again. The surfer drops his rear foot to the tail of his board and pushes down on the left rail. This banks the board to the left and starts it swinging back around toward the break of the wave. As the board swings around, the surfer accelerates the momentum by leaning with the turn-back and maintaining a carving track (path of surfboard).

As the turn-back is completed the surfer drives his board down the face of the wave and out in front of the slope of the wave to execute a bottom turn maneuver. This bottom turn might not have quite so much carve and banking as the initial bottom turn depending on the speed of the turn-back and drive to the bottom. If it is a slower turn, the surfer may arch his back and rise with the flow of the current up the face of the wave, rather than carving up to the top. At any rate, the surfer will once again be in position to re-establish trim across the face of the building wave. The results of the turn-back and bottom turn "S" maneuver will actually leave a trail in an "S" shape on the face of the wave. If by this time the line-up of the wave has built up sufficiently, the surfer will once again start trimming across this face of the wave.

TURN BACK & "S" TURN MANEUVER

1. TURN BACK begins with surfer trimming high in wave, approaching the shoulder.

2. DROPPING REAR FOOT to tail of board, surfer begins to bank into turn back.

3. BOARD SWINGS AROUND, and surfer carves back across shoulder toward break.

4. SURFER DRIVES board to bottom of shoulder and under white water.

5. AT BOTTOM OF WAVE surfer begins bottom turn maneuver.

6. TURNING FROM TAIL — board swings around and banks up face of shoulder.

7. SURFER ARCHES — out of turn to retain speed and climb to top of wave.

8. "S" MANEUVER TRAIL is left on face of wave as surfer completes turning.

Cutbacks . . . TurnBacks . . .

Original Malibu "Hotdogger" Johnny Fain demonstrates an early '60's drop knee CUTBACK.

Towards the mid-late '60's, most cutbacks were performed with both feet firmly planted on the tailblock. Nat Young, Ocean Beach World Contest 1966

Both feet planted firmly on the tail block has worked well on short boards since the early '70's. Mike Purpus, Malibu

Photos from Jamie Budge's "The Living Curl" and "The Californians".

Bottom Turns, Top Turns ... Climbing and Dropping

It is at this section of wave that CLIMBING & DROPPING may be most effective. This is started with a standard bottom turn to the top of the wave. At the top of the wave the surfer then starts to execute a turn back, but instead of turning back, the surfer just turns down to the bottom of the wave without changing wave direction or losing trim in the wave direction. This is followed by another bottom turn climb and a turn-back drop. This series of maneuvers can be used most advantageously by climbing into steep pockets of the wave and gaining optimum speed when driving down out of them with the turn-back drop. This combined series of turning maneuvers is representative of a whole sector of surfing theory and approach which focuses primarily on the turning aspect of surfing over all other forms of positioning and maneuvering.

TRIMMING & STALLING

The art of trimming was established early in the history of surfing by riders of long heavy surfboards. Trimming the board was their method of working their way across the face of the wave. Turning these longer heavier boards was in no way like the radical maneuvers possible on shorter light-weight surfboards. Turning was an arduous task that could only be attempted at the most select of wave situations. These maneuvers sometimes included the dragging of hands, the dropping of the rear knee to the deck of the board and any assorted impromptu inspiration that would propel the board in the desired direction.

With the board going basically in the desired direction, the surfer was most concerned with the weight placement necessary to keep the board moving smoothly across the wave. Although these positionings were developed on longer boards, they are just as applicable and advantageous on shorter boards; even though the trimming point and the turning point may be one and the same.

The surfer begins trimming when he comes out of his bottom turn. As he turns, he is mostly working from the tail of his board, at least in relationship to the carving area of his board. As the surfer gains speed along the track set by the turn, he must shift his weight forward to retain the speed. At first he may merely be leaning forward to accomplish this. As he carves to higher position on the wave, he must actually move forward on his board

TRIMMING & STALLING

① SURFER BEGINS TRIMMING when he comes off the bottom from his first turn.

② MOVING FORWARD on his board, surfer maintains speed developed from turn.

③ IN PERFECT TRIM, surfboard knifes across wave with clean trail.

④ ON NOSE IN TRIM adds style and speed to excellent positioning.

⑤ APPROACHING SHOULDER, surfer moves back on board to slow his speed.

⑥ SURFER STALLS in curl to wait for break to build up in front of him.

⑦ BREAK BUILDS UP and surfer carves turn for speed.

⑧ BACK IN TRIM, surfer moves forward to regain speed across breaking face.

Trimming . . . and Stalling . . .

TRIM usually refers to the place on your board where you can stand and do nothing else to go as fast as possible.

You usually STALL by putting weight on the tailblock to slow the speed of your board. Here, Jay Riddle stalls his board so completely at the top of the wave that he side slips down the face.

SHORT BOARDS - may be impossible to "trim" across small waves. So most surfers hop, skip, jump, gyrate and bounce them across flat sections of the surf.   Jamie Budge, Sunset Blvd.

Images from Jamie Budge, "The Californians".

43

Trimming and Stalling

to set good trim. The object of trim is to set the speed of the board across the face of the wave. A board in good trim will leave a narrow thin trail as it slices across the wave. Moving forward and placing one foot in a "hanging five" position will many times increase the speed of the board to maximum potential for trimming. And besides, hanging five looks provocative.

As the surfer approaches the shoulder at maximum speed, he is in danger of overshooting the slowing break of the wave. At this time, he begins to move back on the board to slow his speed. A further extreme of this is stalling, where the surfer sets a pivoting position on the tail of his board. With proper balance, this can bring the board to a dead halt across the face of the wave. This allows the break to catch up with the surfer as he hangs in limbo pivoting on the tail of his board to retain the stall. As the break builds up again, the surfer can regain speed by carving out of the stall with a turning maneuver and re-setting trim by moving forward on his board. A constant maintenance of trimming positions will not only place the surfer in perfect position across the breaking wave, but also give him optimum advantage in setting up for the various turning maneuvers.

NOSE RIDES & FIN RELEASE

Nose riding is sort of a combination of trimming and stalling. This is because the board is in a trimming position across the face of the wave; but because of the wave positioning involved, the board is more or less "hanging" in place rather than slicing in trim. To begin a nose ride, the surfer usually starts out by putting his board at the top of the wave with a turning maneuver. Once at the top of the wave and angling more or less across the top of the swell, the surfer moves forward on his board to the nose. With one foot over, he starts to push the nose of the board down over in front of the swell. In this way, a nose ride is a combination of riding the face of the wave and the swell also.

As the surfer angles across the wave on the nose, he is "hanging" in place by the tail of his board, planing in the swell. This can be an eerie sensation because it looks like and feels like the surfer is riding in the impossible position; almost walking on water. This "hanging" position of a nose ride is a very precarious one, and can only be maintained as long as he maintains the pitch and steepness necessary.

Should the wave become too slow, the nose ride will become too mushy. If the wave gets too hollow, the board may unhook from the swell altogether and fall sideways down the face, resulting in probable wipeout. The surfer who doesn't wipe out is probably controlling this unhooking action in a side slip fin release. This is achieved when the surfer in a nose ride position pushes down and out with his back foot and actually pushes or allows the fin to fall out of the wave.

As the fin un-hooks, the board will lose most of its forward momentum and the tail of the board will slip sideways down the face. The surfer, still on the nose, will control this side-slip from a see-sawing pivot position where the nose section of the board will have the only functional contact with the face of the wave. When the fin drops all the way down the face, it will once again catch in the bottom of the wave and the board will again regain a forward direction. By this time the surfer should have moved his position toward the middle or tail of the board so as to be prepared to turn or trim as the situation requires.

The nose ride and fin release maneuvers in surfing are both very precarious balances requiring correct waves, advanced skills and perfect timing. The chances are that if a surfer should go to the nose of his board to side slip down the face of a hollow 8 to 10 foot wave, that he and his board are going to find themselves taking separate mid-air courses in free flight down to the bottom. Insult can be added to injury when that ten foot of breaking wave comes pummeling down on top of both. Most surfers therefore, reserve nose riding and fin releases for small waves and playful conditions.

Nose Rides . . .

David Nuuhiwa, nose riding icon of the '60's, Huntington Beach

Miki Dora, mid-spinner on the nose. Malibu

Sometimes the fin will slip out of the wave, requiring extra skill and agility not to wipe out. Jay Riddle, Topanga

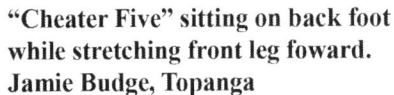

"Cheater Five" sitting on back foot while stretching front leg foward. Jamie Budge, Topanga

Jamie Budge shoots movies of his own feet with hand-held camera. Malibu.

46   Images from "The Living Curl" and "The Californians"

NOSE RIDES
FIN RELEASE

1. NOSE RIDE BEGINS as surfer turns toward top of wave.

2. AT TOP OF WAVE surfer moves to nose of board and pushes down face.

3. BOARD DROPS down face into trimming position. Surfer holds nose ride.

4. AS WAVE GETS TOO STEEP or too slow, surfer moves back to maintain good trim.

5. FIN RELEASE BEGINS if surfer pushes tail of board down and out of wave.

6. FIN WILL THEN SIDE SLIP down face of wave as surfer pivots on nose.

7. FIN WILL CATCH at bottom of wave as surfer moves back on surfboard.

8. REGAINING TRIM is accomplished as board once again picks up forward momentum.

KICK OUT—ROLLER COASTER

The kick-out is a turning maneuver to propel a surfer out over the top of a breaking wave to avoid disaster in the close-out. *A roller coaster* is first half-kick-out and second half-turn-back over with the break of the wave. The up and down of this maneuver accounts for the amusement park name.

The surfer begins to set up for the kick-out when he observes that he is heading into a close-out section. At this time, he banks his board down to the bottom of the wave to set up for a turn. At the bottom of the wave, the surfer carves hard up the face of the wave in a bottom turn maneuver. Only instead of coming out of the turn into trim, he comes out of the turn out over the top of the wave to exit before the wave closes out.

Sometimes this can take the surfer out of the wave with great speed and height, as in a "fly-away" pull-out. In this situation, the surfer actually shoots out over the top of the wave and several feet into mid-air. It is then up to the surfer while in mid-air to either grab onto his board so as to come down with it, or separate from it so it does not come down on him. Anyway, the surfer is out of the wave. If he wishes not to exit the wave, then he does a roller coaster maneuver.

This begins at the top of the wave just after the kick-out bottom turn. Only instead of shooting out over the top of the wave, the surfer executes a turn-back approach at the top of the wave. If his timing is correct with the breaking lip of the wave, this turn-back will shoot him back over into mid-air with the break. He will experience sort of a launching, flying sensation when going over the falls with the break. This can be one of the most dynamic and exciting maneuvers in surfing, with the timing and quickness of the maneuver giving a burst of rocket-like speed and actual blast-off. After a split second in mid-air with the break, the surfer should touch down at the bottom of the wave still on his feet prepared to finish out the ride in the white water.

The kick-out, of course, is a maneuver that every surfer masters for his own protection in difficult surfing conditions. *The roller coaster* can be a little extravagant at times, but always impressive and exciting. The novice should immediately find some method of exiting difficult waves, and practice the fancy stuff at his leisure in predictable time and conditions.

KICKOUT

(1) KICK OUT BEGINS when surfer realizes that he is heading into a close-out section.

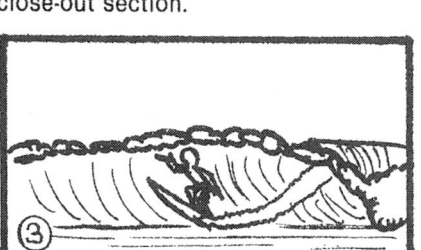

(3) AT BOTTOM of wave, surfer carves into hard turn up face of wave.

(5A) KICK OUT ENDS with surfer safely over the break of the wave grabbing his board.

(6) ROLLER COASTER ENDS with surfer touching down in the whitewater.

ROLLER COASTER

(2) SURFER DRIVES to bottom of wave for position for kick out.

(4) OVER THE TOP with momentum from turn, surfer avoids the breaking lip.

(5B) ROLLER COASTER BEGINS if surfer decides to turn back over with break of wave.

(7) MID AIR breaking with the wave, surfer free falls toward the bottom.

KickOut... Roller Coaster... or...

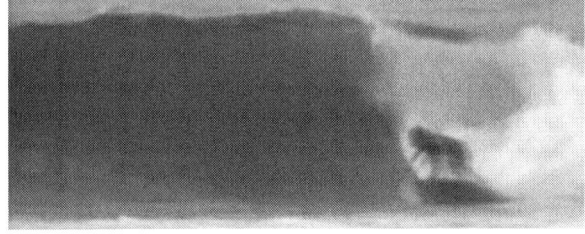

CLIMB and DROP

CARVE - Hard off bottom.

CLIMB - Up face...
for fly-away kick out
or Get Air
or ...

... KICK OUT of wave.   Or turn back over with break.   And DROP back in ...

CARVE Hard off bottom (again).

ENJOY - the rest of your ride.

Angie Reno, Malibu
Images from Jamie Budge's "The Californians"

50

CURL RIDES

Curl rides, or tube rides are the ultimate in the surfing experience. Not only is riding in the tube the most precarious of all surfing positions, requiring exceptional timing and board position, but it is the most thrilling of all sensations in that the surfer is seemingly completely enveloped by the wave. This is accomplished when the surfer positions himself in the hollow between the face of the wave and the breaking curl or lip. He is then in the tunnel, the hot spot, the green room, the eye of the hurricane or whatever the local surfers are calling it this week.

To get in that particular position, the surfer begins by slowing his board down with a stalling position. If he is riding the right kind of hollow wave, he will then be waiting for the curl to catch up with him from behind and break over him. At the point when he can spot the breaking curl about to come over him, he tucks into a crouch to insure that his body area will fit completely into the tunnel. In this method, by stalling his speed, he can place himself further and further back in the tube for a prolonged period of time or until he experiences nervous collapse. Because the surfer is riding with the threat of wipe-out literally all around him, the tube ride can be as threatening as it is exhilarating.

Most surfers, once in the tube, will concentrate their efforts on getting back out of the tunnel. This is done by moving or leaning forward to increase speed to out-race the break of the curl and once again emerge to the open face of the wave. He may then feel confident enough to try for another tube ride, or may go on to some other phase of wave riding.

The tube ride, even though it is one of the most thrilling of surfing experiences, is not all that difficult for the novice to attempt. On the appropriate curling wave, he need only turn his board and wait, and then crouch as the wave breaks over him. Getting in the tube is not difficult, it is the riding in the tube and the getting back out again that is the hard part. This comes only with experience and ability, so attempt your first curl rides in very controlled uncrowded conditions, where you won't have to swim very far.

Curl Rides... Tube Rides...

Rick Irons, Oceanside Invitational

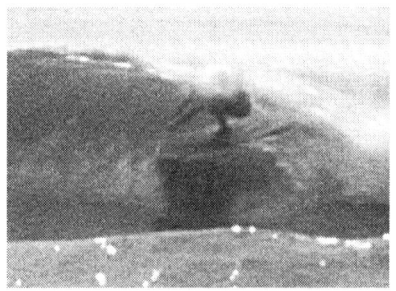

Jamie Budge, Stanley's

If you stall (slow down) in the curl... you can get coverd by the tube.

John Peck, covered up at Hammonds Reef

Davey Hilton, Pt. Dume

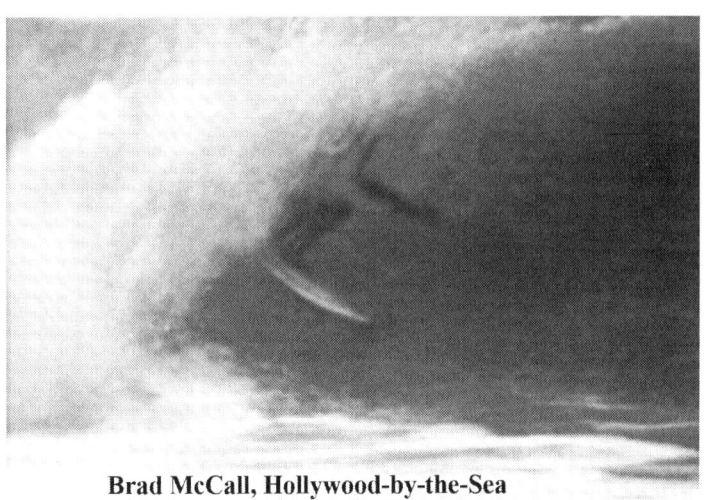

Brad McCall, Hollywood-by-the-Sea

Photos from Jamie Budge's "The Living Curl" and "The Californians"

CURL RIDES... TUBE RIDES...

CURL RIDE BEGINS as surfer slows board to wait for curl to pass him.

SURFER TUCKS into crouch as curl breaks over him.

IN THE TUBE surfer rides in hollow between face and breaking curl of wave.

DRIVING TO OPEN WATER, surfer emerges from tube and carves into trim.

CURL RIDE FROM WATER ANGLE begins as surfer slows board to wait for curl.

SURFER tucks into crouch as curl breaks over him.

IN THE TUBE, surfer rides in hollow between face and breaking curl of wave.

DRIVING TO OPEN WATER, surfer emerges from tube and carves into trim.

BACK SIDE APPROACH

Surfing back-side is difficult to explain, partially because it is done the same as surfing frontside, only different. Like playing tennis with your left hand if you're right-handed, you want to do all the same things but have to go about it differently. Most accomplished backside surfers appear to ride the waves in a semi-crouched stance. This is to off-set the normal tendency to lean forward and to give the surfer the needed weight positioning on the inside rail where the turning and planing will take place.

In coming off the bottom of a bottom turn the surfer will sometimes crouch so much his own bottom is dragging in the wave. This is representative of the weight displacement necessary to turn the board with the necessary banking and speed. In gaining speed out of the turn, the surfer (although leaning backward into the wave) will lean and move forward on his board to maintain speed and set trim. To maintain trim and sometimes to stablilize back-side nose rides, the surfer may grab the rail of his board and hang on through difficult sections. Upon coming to a shoulder, all the front-side reactions can be brought into full play for a split second as the surfer turns back toward the break and for an instant is facing the wave he is riding. At the bottom of the wave, he must once again shift to back-side technique for a bottom turn to complete the "S" maneuver and establish wave direction.

Many of the other surfing maneuvers such as trimming and stalling, surf rides, nose rides, fin releases, climbing and dropping, etc., are done with the same set-ups as frontside, but with the crouched-over, back-to-the-wave, back-side approach with the balance on the inside rail. A back-side kick-out or roller coaster can give the surfer a distinct advantage once he has turned up to the lip of the wave, in that when he comes back over with the break, he will be facing the direction in which he is going. In fact many of the backside situations have a distinct advantage over the parallel front-side situation. Because of this, many surfers consider back-side a separate art in surfing itself, with the riders gearing their techniques to take advantage of the opportunities available only on a backside wave.

These opportunities might include the radical climbing and dropping possible, the off-the-lip roller coaster, the radical turn-back and the rail-grab nose-ride. The advantage in these set-ups comes from the fact that the surfer is facing a different part of the wave than would be possible on a front-side situation. Novices going back-side should have no trouble merely riding back-side waves. The differences will be apparent in the maneuvering, and the mastering of the techniques will come with practice and experience.

CLIMB & DROP
AND BACKSIDE APPROACH

① CLIMBING & DROPPING BEGINS as surfer banks off bottom of wave into steep section.

② AT TOP OF SECTION surfer breaks almost completely out of wave.

③ TURNING BACK at top of wave, surfer changes direction back down wave.

④ DRIVING TOWARD BOTTOM, surfer completes maneuver and heads into another series.

① BACKSIDE BOTTOM TURN is done back-to-wave, carving upward in turnback fashion.

② IN TRIM ON NOSE, surfer may grab rail of board for extra backside stability.

③ TURN BACK and "S" MANEUVER require top turn, driving, and backside bottom turn.

④ BACKSIDE ROLLER COASTER lets surfer come over front side with break of wave.

55

Backside Bottom Turns

... and Off-the-Lip

Longboard drop-knee backside bottom turn. John Peck Salt Creek, circa 1966

Shortboard backside bottom turn with both feet planted on tailblock. Mike Purpus, Redondo Breakwater

Mike Off-the-Lip Backside. Although "getting air" hadn't been invented yet, it happened. Mike Purpus below ...

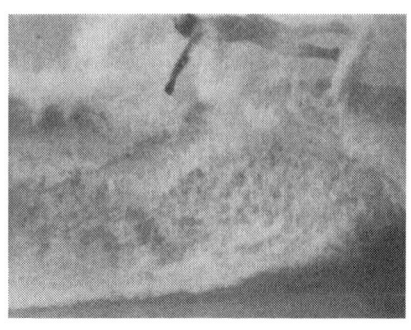

Photos from Jamie Budge's "The Living Curl" and "The Californians"

RIGHT WAVE COMPLETE

Now that you know all that can be done on any given wave, here is a brief description of how one particular surfer might handle one particular wave:

Taking off at the initial peak of a long right breaking line-up, the surfer drops down the face driving his board to the bottom. Hitting the bottom of the wave, he carves his board to the right, banking up the wave just ahead of the fast breaking curl. Coming off the bottom he is faced with a fast breaking section. He moves forward on his board for speed and crouches so as to tuck himself under the breaking curl. A few seconds later, he has beat the curl and reached the shoulder of the wave. At this point, he rises to the top of the wave and turns back hard and drives left and down the face under the whitewater. And once again, he does another turn off the bottom of the shoulder to place him in the appropriate wave direction.

Coming out of the bottom turn, he is moving into the inside line-up, the smaller portion of the break, where he can try some fun maneuvers. As the line builds up, he puts himself in fast trim and he stretches out to "hang five" over the nose. He hits an unexpected hollow spot and he finds his fin releasing from the wave. But he is prepared, and as the fin drops, he catches himself pivoting just back from the nose and controls the fin release. The fin catches at the bottom of the wave, and the surfer carves into a slow trim on the tail and then does some tail block stalling while the curl splits across his waist. At this point, the wave speeds up some, and he does a few short climb and drop turns across this fast section.

Now moving with excellent speed, he finds that he is facing the final close out section. He drives his board down to the bottom of the wave, powers a hard carving turn up the face, breaks through the curling lip of the closeout section, turns back hard and comes over with the break in a roller coaster maneuver. The surfer free-falls down the last few feet of the drop and finishes his ride in the soup as it breaks behind him. From the soup he does a pull-out maneuver over the white water and paddles back out, somewhat excited over his complete ride. He feels a surge of pride as he finds that all the novices in the water have been admiring his work, and he offers them a few words of encouragement to keep practicing.

RIGHT WAVE COMPLETE
EXAMPLE

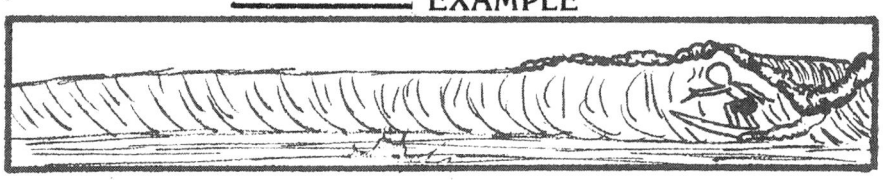

SURFER BEGINS RIDE with bottom turn as wave begins to break behind him.

IN FULL TRIM, surfer tucks into short curl ride with section of break next to initial peak.

AT FIRST SHOULDER, surfer turns back to wait for line to build up in front of him.

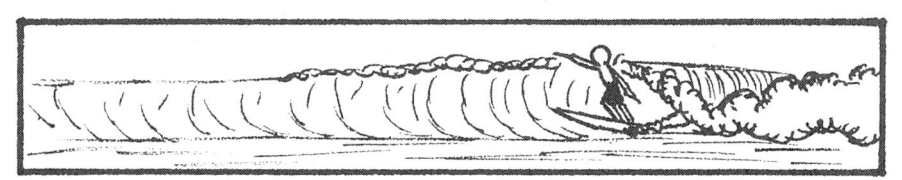

ANOTHER BOTTOM TURN puts surfer once again in trimming position as wave forms into inside line up.

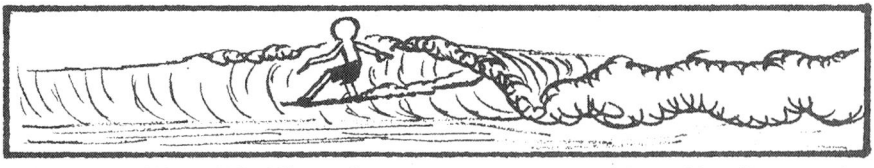

ACROSS INSIDE LINE UP, surfer may execute nose rides, side slips or other maneuvers.

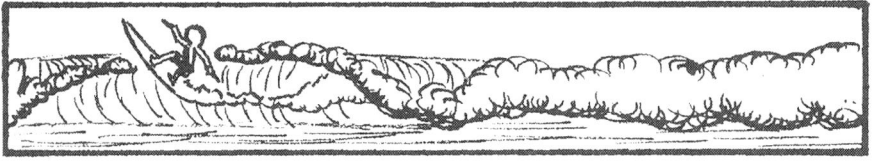

AS WAVE CLOSES OUT, he has the choice of kicking out or turning back for roller coaster to end his ride.

Right Wave Complete an example

Hard bottom turn gets surfer moving away from white water.

But he might have to cut back as wave slows down at shoulder.

As wave builds up in front of him, he might trim or nose ride across face.

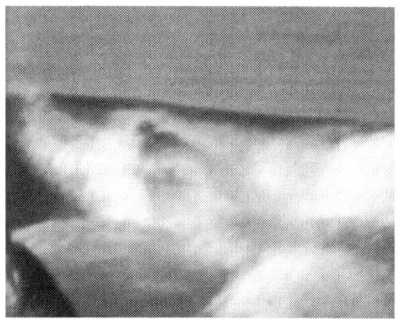

If wave throws out over him, he might get a body dip or tube ride.

If wave slows down, he might turn back again.

Or he might find himself side slipping in a steep section.

If wave closes out, he might have to make a quick kick-out.

Jay Riddle, Topanga,
from Jamie Budge's "The Californians"

LEFT WAVE COMPLETE

That same surfer who has just handled that complete right-breaking to its fullest potential might find himself in a beautifully lining up left-breaking wave. In that situation, the same surfer might handle the wave thus:

Dropping to the bottom of the wave just before the initial peak breaks, the surfer carves a hard backside turn to the left. The banking is so steep that his bottom is almost dragging in the face of the wave. He comes off the bottom with considerable speed and moves slightly forward on his board to maintain that speed and set trim. The initial peak of the wave has turned into a fast breaking section and the surfer crouches so as to tuck under the curl. Coming out of the curl, he approaches the first shoulder, rises up the top of the wave and cuts back hard toward the break of the wave (to the right) and drives down underneath the soup. At the bottom of the wave, he executes another back-side bottom turn and re-sets his wave direction. Coming out of this turn, he faces the faster inside line-up. He moves to the nose of his board, crouches down and grabs his outside rail for stability.

While trimming in nose-ride position across this section, he realizes that he is approaching the final close out of the wave. Sizing up the close-out and adjusting his timing, he drops to the bottom of the wave and carves a hard turn up the face. Shooting back-side up the wave, he bursts through the breaking lip of the wave and turns back over with the curl. Facing in the direction of his turn-back, he drops over free fall with the break of the wave in a roller coaster and hits the bottom to finish his ride in the white water.

Paddling back out the line-up, he contemplates his back-side technique of primary weight over the inside rail, and crouched-over stance for necessary control of the back-side approach.

LEFT WAVE COMPLETE
EXAMPLE

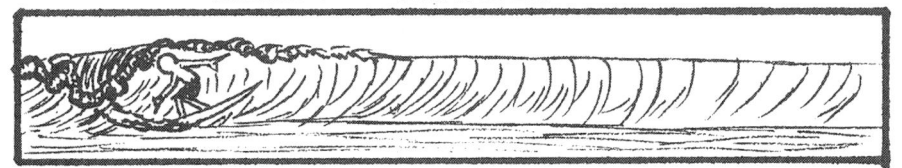

SURFER BEGINS BACKSIDE WAVE with bottom turn to gain speed away from initial break of wave.

CROUCHING BACKSIDE, surfer tucks under tight section following initial peak.

SURFER TURNS BACK OFF TOP as curl slows down at first shoulder.

ANOTHER BACKSIDE BOTTOM TURN puts surfer in trimming position across inside line of wave.

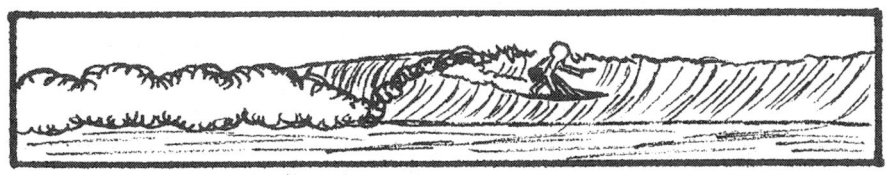

TRIMMING ON THE NOSE, he grabs the rail of his board for stability and to maintain speed.

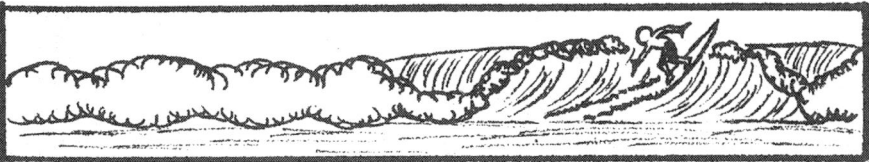

AS WAVE CLOSES OUT, surfer can pull out over top or turn back into roller coaster to end ride in white water.

LEFT WAVE COMPLETE
Backside, Longboard Example

Backside Bottom Turn

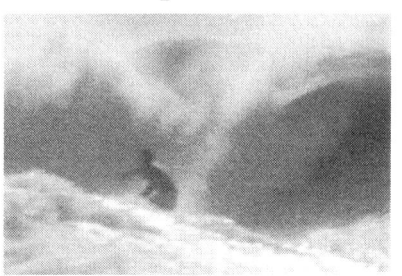

Trim under Tube

Crouch in Curl

Turnback, Cutback at shoulder

Backside Turn at Shoulder

Trim across shoulder

Noseride at shoulder

Kickout at end of wave

Richard Roche at Hollywood-by-the-Sea from "The Living Curl"
Photo © Jamie Budge

OTHER MANEUVERS

Other maneuvers in surfing that are considered less functional, but nevertheless get some degree of utilization are:

The head dip, which is a curl ride in which the only part of your body that rides in the curl is your head. This is executed by leaning over and dunking your head in the wave.

Hanging Ten, is a nose ride with both feet so close to the nose that all ten toes hang over the end. Usually about as functional as hanging five toes over the nose.

The tail block side-slip, actually a functional stalling maneuver. The surfer releases the fin from the wave while standing on the tailblock of his board, slips sideways down the face of the wave.

The 360 degree spin, an exaggerated side-slip maneuver where the board spins completely around in a full circle while the surfer pivots in the middle of his board.

The 360 degree turn, an excellent maneuver but you'll probably never see one. Extremely difficult to execute, the surfer turns his board in a complete circle on the face of the wave. Sort of a "loop-the-loop" of surfing.

Spinner, not even a board maneuver, the surfer turns a complete circle bodily on his board as it trims across the wave. A good maneuver for novices who wish to believe they can do those 360 degree maneuvers.

Fly-Away Kick Out, is a manuever where the surfer kicks his board high in the sky when pulling out of the wave. Functional, in that the board is sure to fly to safety (or at another surfer). Unfunctional in that the surfer must swim whatever distance is necessary to recover his board.

Skeg First Take-Off, about as functional as driving your car backwards down the freeway in reverse. Surfer takes off on the wave with his board going backwards, skeg-first. Once in the wave, the fin catches and the board flips around to go front first in the right direction.

Riding Surfboard Up-Side Down, Fin Up, actually functional. If you happen to be surfing in three inches of water over jagged rock bottom. Otherwise, watch out that you don't stab yourself with your fin.

Riding Surfboard With No Fin, great for long out-of-control ride sideways in the white water. Or an uncontrollable series of 360 degree spins.

63

Other Manuvers   Creative Surfing

Most of these "manuvers" have nothing to do with making the board do much of anything constructive on the wave. But they are fun and showey antics.

Duo Tandem Quasimodo
Miki Dora, Micky Munoz

Backwards Prone Pushup Leg-Lift
Corky Carroll

Fin-First Take Off
Ron Sizemore

Difficult 360 Degree Fin Spin,
Board Spin.   Jay Riddle

Riding two surfboards at the same time. Johnny Fain (steps onto Steve Bigler's board).

Walking backwards (or forwards towards the back of the board).
Dru Harrison

Other Maneuvers

Neat Surfing Stances, like "Hood Ornament," standing on your board in a position like a fancy hood ornament on a car; or *"Quasimoto,"* standing hunched over; or any other character that you can identify with from your favorite comic book. Mostly these stances have nothing whatsoever to do with the actual sport of surfing, but sometimes the friendly gargoyles on the beach will give you a nod of recognition for a well executed "neat surfing stance." Aside from the maneuvers listed here that are either functional or useless, you will find that there are new ones being invented every day, or at least new names being used for old maneuvers. This will require a certain amount of study on the part of the novice surfer to be sure that he is relating in the appropriate terms.

ADVICE ON MANEUVERING

Probably the best word of advice on learning the basic maneuvers in surfing, is to keep practicing. The novice attempting new maneuvers for the first time may find them somewhat difficult. However, the reward is in the successful execution of such maneuvers. The first time that you do a well performed bottom turn or place yourself perfectly in the tunnel, the accompanying thrill should be enough to carry you on to better turns and more tunnel rides. The problem, of course, is to get yourself over the hump of beginning to learn these maneuvers to the point where enthusiasm takes over from the excitement of better surfing.

In attempting maneuvers for the first times, it can be helpful to study the surfers whose styles seem to be closest to your own. By forming pictures in your mind of their particular turning style when attempting your own, you will find your turning beginning to work with the same effectiveness of theirs. One maneuver, such as a bottom turn, can be practiced over and over on one good wave, until the intricacies of such a maneuver are all coordinated for their best effectiveness. But the motivation for good surfing must come from the individual. The descriptions and techniques discussed in this book can only be a guideline to which the surfer applies his own efforts, experimentations and practice. Therefore, get yourself out in the water, catch as many waves as you can, and start practicing those maneuvers.

MANEUVERING IN CONTESTS

Contests in surfing are one way of comparing one surfer's style and ability against other surfers. As maneuvering is the basis of surfing ability, most of these contests have a point system of rating these maneuvers. Surfing contests are held in "heats" of about 4 to 6 surfers in the water at one time. These surfers catch from three to six waves (or sometimes more) in a given period of time, usually between 15 and 30 minutes.

The rides they get are scored by judges on the beach who give them points based on their ability and the handling of the waves they catch. The points range on a scale from one to ten, one being the lowest and ten being the highest. A surfer taking off on a wave will be evaluated by the judges and given a number of points. The surfer with the most points wins the heat and goes on to the next heat or the final heats. A surfer catching the biggest and best waves of the heat and performing a series of fast, accurate maneuvers will usually get a 9 or 10. Catching smaller waves with one or two good maneuvers and a lot of cruising will usually earn a surfer between 5 and 7 points. A surfer who wipes out on a wave, or takes off on a close-out will get between 1 and 4 points depending on what happens before disaster hits.

The major problem for a surfer in a contest, is getting the biggest and best waves to perform on. Here, experience and wave judgment are a prerequisite for good points. The surfer first in the wave and next to the curl has wave possession and any others interfering will be docked in points. The other major problem for a competing surfer is his ability to perform under the pressure of time and other contestants. Where a surfer may be able to perform certain maneuvers on his own free time, under the pressure of a contest, these manuevers may not come off. Therefore, most competing surfers have a repertoire of standard maneuvers which they can perform well at any time, and let the exceptional maneuvers happen exceptionally.

It is interesting that although many of the best surfers come up consistently on top in contests; there is always that element of the right 'novice' in the right place at the right time to win some contests where it is completely unexpected. It is this element of the unexpected that keeps surfing contests an exciting showplace for new talent. As a novice increases his ability, he may find contests a rewarding experience towards furthering his effective surfing.

RIDING BIG SURF

The experience of riding big surf is quite a bit different from riding small "fun" surf. Many professional surfers gear either a part or their whole scope toward the effective riding of larger waves. This involves the special design of "big gun" surfboards and a careful, thorough study of swell directions, current conditions and bottom configurations of the big wave spots that they ride. Physical conditioning must be at optimum, and most big wave riders will ride only in the company of other experienced big wave riders to the exclusion of unproven novices.

How large is "large surf" depends on who is calling out the numbers. What looks to be fifty foot to the novice may be ten foot to the pro. Most big wave riders judge the size of the wave by the height of the swell and not the face of the wave. Hence the actual size may be one-half to two-thirds the appearance of the face.

Paddling out in big surf calls for knowing the surfing location, studying where the break is and watching how often sets are coming through. The object is to time the paddling in between sets of waves so the surfer can make it out through a channel to the line-up without endangering himself or interfering with surfers who may be riding. The finding of deep water channels where even the biggest sets are not breaking may be essential to getting out to the line-up. The line-up in big surf can be quite scary due to the many different places a larger wave may appear to break before it actually does.

At many reef breaks, the swells will peak up outside, cap over in a false break, back off, take a right turn and seem to be heading crosswise across the line-up and at the last moment switch direction and break over the reef in a perfect tunnel. The novice surfer experiencing this for the first time may be paddling all over the ocean in a state of panic trying to avoid being cleaned up. Fortunately, the wave never breaks until it hits the spot where all the experienced surfers have been calmly waiting for it. The lesson is "know the line-up." This will take some homework on the beach, studying the waves and talking to locals, but it is worth the effort. Paddling for and catching the wave also has a different approach in big waves. Where a late take-off with a few lazy strokes may be casual in small surf, it may be disastrous in the heavies.

The conservative approach in big surf would be to get into the wave early before it starts to feather or curl at the top. The surfer should be well on his way, "taking the drop," before it starts to break.

Big Surf . . .

Rolf Arness carves backside off bottom of whitewater shoulder at Waimea Bay.

Big surf can toss, tumble and exhaust you.
Beware of strong forces at work.
from Hal Jepsen's footage in Jamie Budge's "The Californians".

Riding Big Surf

Taking the drop should be a driving race to the bottom for optimum speed so that the following bottom turn will be most effective in gaining speed across the wave direction. Any slip-up, such as waiting too long to drop in, or hanging too high on the face, may end up with a launch over the falls with the break. It is also interesting to note that, while dropping in at the shoulder of the wave may seem safer or easier, it may be dangerous.

Because of the power of the initial break, and the massive movement of the water in the swell, the shoulder may be the worst place to drop in. This is because it is very easy to get hung up trying to drop into the massive but mushy shoulder while the break of the wave comes charging across the face to wipe out the surfer before he is even really into the wave. This plus violent karate chops from any surfer already riding the wave ought to be enough to deter the novice from shoulder hopping.

If the surfer takes off with the initial break of the wave and drives down the face, he will be in the best position for a good bottom turn and the resulting advantages of speed gained. Where a turn on a smaller wave may be a mere flip of the board, on the heavies it is going to be a deep penetrating carve with studied momentum throughout the maneuver. Too much carve and the fin is going to unhook, too little carve and he is not going to gain any speed. While turning, the surfer will not only be dealing with the direction he wishes to go, but also with a forceful rush of water of "up-draft" up the face of the wave, caused by the movement of the massive swell. This up-draft will cause much of the surfer's planing to be against this forward motion, and allow him to hold his penetrating turn for an extended period of time.

When coming out of the turn and establishing trim, the surfer will once again encounter this, the up-draft of water up the face. He may find that he will be trimming as much across this current as he will be across the face of the wave. This may make the angle of trim in certain places as little as forty-five degrees across the line-up. This also has an influence on turn-backs (and all maneuvers). The turn-back may change the surfers direction, but after that he will once again be driving down across the up-draft to get back in position for turning. If he does not constantly work with his wave direction and speed, the surfer may find that he stagnates, or comes to a place where he can't angle across the face of the wave. He may feel like he is going a million miles an hour due to the rush of the up-draft, but in reality he is not getting anywhere, and it will be only seconds before the break overtakes him. Do not lose speed or wave direction. It will be hard to re-establish.

69

RIDING BIG SURF

PADDLING OUT — must be through rip tides or channels where even the biggest set waves do not break. Paddling should be timed to be in between sets of waves.

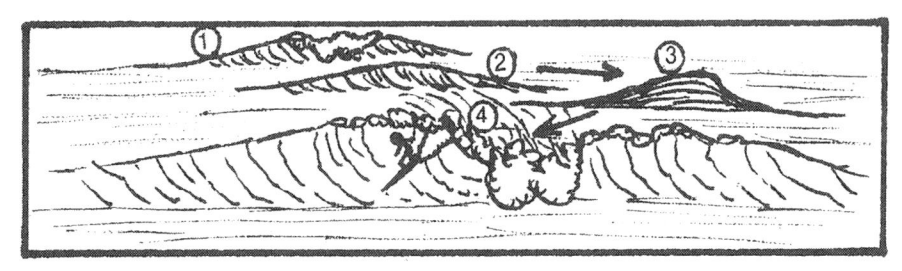

THE LINE UP — in big surf can be tricky. 1 swell peaks outside. 2 swell reforms. 3 swell takes radical shift to right. 4 swell shifts left and breaks. Lesson: know your line up.

THE TAKE OFF — should be early before the wave breaks. Surfer drives down face of wave early to avoid getting "hung up" in break of wave.

BOTTOM TURN — is deep penetrating carve at bottom of wave to set trim direction and speed. Maneuver should be extended as long as possible for maximum forward momentum.

RIDING BIG SURF

"UP DRAFT" — affects trimming in big surf. 1 surfer trims at 45 degree angle across face and up draft. 2 surfer has lost wave direction in up-draft and will be wiped out.

UP DRAFT AFFECTS ALL MANEUVERS — as with the turn back, surfer performs maneuver and then must drive down face of wave (and up draft) in order to re-establish wave direction.

POSITIONING MUST BE PLANNED IN ADVANCE — to beat difficult sections. 1 surfer turns off bottom early to 2 get high in wave to beat "bowl" section building up ahead.

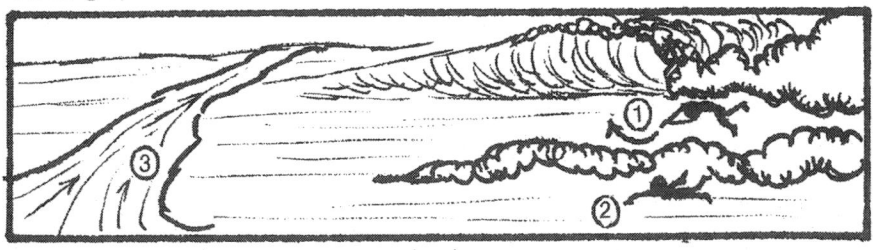

SURFERS STAY WITH WHITE WATER AFTER WIPEOUT. 1 surfer dives under set wave to avoid turbulence. 2 surfer stays with soup and body surfs to shore. 3 both avoid rip tide channel which could carry them out to sea.

Riding Big Surf

With all this going on at once, the surfer will also have to plan his maneuvers and positioning in advance. On a small wave where the surfer may whip up to the top of the curl with a flick of the knees, on big surf this is not the case. He may have to plan 15 seconds in advance to be at the top of the wave and driving down across a difficult "bowl." If he doesn't, he may be so far behind it that he will get squashed. And wipe-outs in heavy surf may be little or no fun at all.

Aside from these various specifics of large surf, one must also be impressed by the overall impact of the conditions. Everything is intensified: waves are bigger, surfers are going faster, slip-ups are more dangerous, tempers are quicker, and stupidity will not be tolerated by anyone. Outside sets can clean up every surfer in the water, rip tides can carry you miles out to sea, and a breaking wave can break your back. Be advised that only the foolish will take these circumstances lightly. Do not get into conditions that you cannot handle. Be most cautious in any big wave situation. Observe all previously mentioned rules of the road and advice on wipe-outs.

If you do get wiped out, don't panic, or fight the wipe out. You will be under water for a while, but it will pass. Struggling will only waste your air and energy. Stay in the white water and let the breaking waves wash you to shore. When the sets come and you are swimming, dive under the wave. In some clear water conditions, you can look up and see when the wave and turbulence has passed and it is safe to surface. Otherwise, dive down, swim under and surface when you estimate the wave has passed. Relax and move easily toward the shore with the waves. In a few moments you will be on the beach and storing up a second wind for another try.

APPROACH TO PIPELINES

A "pipeline" is a hollow breaking wave which forms a pipe shaped effect when breaking. The wave is so hollow that it actually leaves a round tunnel or pipe between the face and the break of the wave. Because of this extremely forceful wave breaking in very shallow water, an entirely different approach to riding pipelines is used than with other more normal surf. The surfer's main effort is concentrated on keeping his board hooked to the radically steep face of the wave. All turning maneuvers are performed with maximum caution as the surfer is more concerned with his position and speed across tubing pipeline.

On the take-off, the surfer is dealing with a wave that will probably be unridable until the very last second when the swell hits a shallow reef. This causes the take-off to be late, steep and as close to a free fall drop as one would want to experience. The main effort is for the surfer to get down the face of the wave before the break takes him over the falls with it. When the surfe reaches the bottom, the wave will already be tubing over on top of him. At this point the bottom turn will be very critical. Because of the sucking of water up the face and the steepness at the bottom of the wave, the surfer cannot exert a lot of effort in the maneuver. He must bank his board cautiously and let the sucking force of the wave propel him in the desired direction. In coming out of the turn, he must ride high enough to avoid the tubing break now hitting the bottom of the wave, but not too high where his find might unhook in the steepness of the face. At this point, he begins to establish his trim and wave position across the "pipeline." His weight must be focused on the inside rail to compensate for the sucking force, and he must be constantly shifting and adjusting to find the spot on the face that is steep enough to maintain speed but not so steep as to fall out of the wave.

Now comes the whole point of riding "pipelines"; riding inside the tube itself. Because of the piping shape of the wave, surfers spend more time in the tube than in any other kind of wave. On many waves, the tube is the safest and only possible route to beating or making a fast pipeline break. To get into the tube, the surfer adjusts his speed of trimming to allow the wave to break just ahead of him. If it is a large tube, he may just stand up straight and look around in awe.

At this point the adrenalin should be pumping full speed. The surfer is surrounded by water sucking up on one side of him, throwing out over his head and avalanching down on the other side of him. He is surrounded by wipe-outs on all sides, yet he hangs safely (if only for the second) in the eye of the hurricane.

Approach to Tube Rides . . .

TAKE OFF - can be steep or free fall.

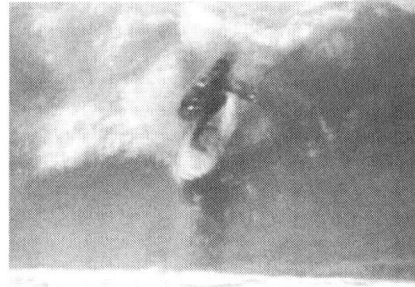

DRIVE to bottom of wave.

CARVE hard off the bottom.

STALL - out of turn.

CROUCH - and let tube overtake you.

COVERED UP - by TUBE which may shoot spray out the tunnel.

EXIT TUBE - and regain speed by turning or trimming on face of wave.

DON'T get sucked over falls. Can be painful and embarrasing.

Brad McCall, Hollywood-by-the-Sea
Images from Jamie Budge's "The Living Curl" and "The Californians"

APPROACH TO "PIPELINES"

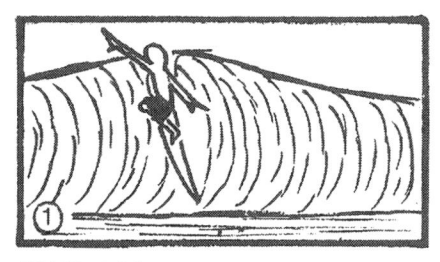

① TAKE OFFS are late and steep. Surfer's main effort is to stay attached to wave.

② FORCE OF WAVE exaggerates surfer's cautious banking at bottom of wave.

③ WEIGHT ON INSIDE RAIL keeps surfer hooked to hollow face while trimming.

④ IN THE PIPE or tube, surfer grabs rail for stability in the hot spot.

⑤ WAVE SPITTING toward end of tunnel can blow surfer out of tube or off his board.

⑥ PULL OUT is important as closeout can be hard and hollow.

AVOID GOING OVER THE FALLS. Waves hit hard in extremely shallow water.

AVOID RIDING TOO HIGH — can cause surfer to unhook from wave and wipeout.

Approach to Pipelines

How long he can remain there before a slip up wipes him out in the havoc all around, depends on his ability. If he gets too low on the wave, the break coming over will get him; too high, and he will fall out of the face; too far back, and the churning mass will get him from behind. The longer the surfer is in the tube, the more critical it becomes to juggle all the variables, and the more anxious he is to get back out.

If all goes well, the tunnel will start to slow down toward the shoulder of the break and allow the surfer to squeek back out. At this point the wave may spit out the tube a blast of spray that has accumulated in the inner depths. This blast or spit may be enough to blow a tube-riding surfer back out of the tube, or off his board, or both. The lesson is to be prepared for it as a lift out of the tunnel, and an indication of the end of the pipeline.

At this point the surfer may find himself at a temporary shoulder. Temporary, because it will most likely be followed by a shallow water crunchy closeout. It is best in this situation for the surfer to make a quick exit kick-out out for the back before the close-out closes out. Now comes the easy part, collapse from over adrenalin excitability as the surfer realized he has been inside the eye of the pipeline and come out to tell about it.

And now that he might be cocky with initial success, it is a good time to remind him of all the dangers. First of all, the whole nature of a pipeline type wave depends on a shallow bottom. This may be a sand bar or a jaggedy coral reef, so if you hit it you may get bounced off the sand or split open on the coral. Do not get hung up at the top of the wave, as you may go over the falls right into that shallow bottom. Do not ride too high as you may fall out of the wave and get sucked over the falls anyway. Avoid taking off with other surfers and watch for a hard close-out at the end of the wave.

Aside from the minor precautions, the pipeline experience can be most thrilling. There are a number of "pipes," including, of course, the Banzai Pipeline, Black's Beach, and some exceptional days at Newport or Santa Ana River Jetty. And one of the most enjoyable "pipelines" may be the one at your own local surf spot, when the swell direction, sand bars and tide all add to perfection tubing right in your own back yard. Wherever the pipeline may be, be prepared for the extra caution and critical positioning necessary for successful riding.

BEACHES, POINTS & REEFS

The types of surfing locations are divided into three major categories: beaches, points and reefs. Even where none of these seem to be present, the result of waves breaking at all indicates one of these types of conditions under the wave.

A BEACH BREAK forms over shifting sandbars that build up from the washing action of the surf. Where these sand bars build up the most, is where the most well-defined waves break. A four foot wave will merely form a swell in eight feet of water. When that same wave hits a sand bar six foot under the water, it will curl over and break in a peak with a right and left break off either side. This is the ideal beach break situation, where surfers can choose from several different peaks breaking up and down the beach. The most experienced surfers will usually have one section of the beach picked out for themselves, but there are almost always uncrowded peaks available to the novices.

Beach breaks can break best on either low or high tide, depending on the beach. Usually, the better the sand bar formation, the better the location will break at low tide. Many beach breaks with poor sand bar formation will break good only at high tide. Almost all beach breaks will blow out to sloppy conditions at the slightest breath of wind. Therefore, they are usually best in the morning before the wind comes up, or late in the afternoon when the wind dies down.

This works out well with the local swimming ordinances which usually prohibit board surfing from about 10 am till 6 pm, especially in the summer. In the winter, off-shore winds may keep beaches ridable all day long. Rains or rare all-day glass-offs can also enhance beach break surfing. Beach breaks are usually the best choice for beginning surfing because the surfer can find uncrowded waves devoid of rocks and other hazards.

REEF BREAKS form over submerged reefs of coral, rocks, old sunken cars, bodies or whatever else a wave may break over. Most reef breaks form far out in the ocean and break best at low tide when the water is shallow over the reef. Usually each reef will have its own pronounced peak and line-up. The best reef breaks have become very well known and seem to be the sole property of the experienced local surfers. However, there are many lesser known reef breaks which can afford excellent learning conditions with easy swelling waves and long predictable rides. Sometimes these waves will be shared with kayaks, catamarans and other larger surfing vessels, but that is usually preferable to the local kamikaze surfers who will hog the other reef breaks.

BEACHES, POINTS & REEFS

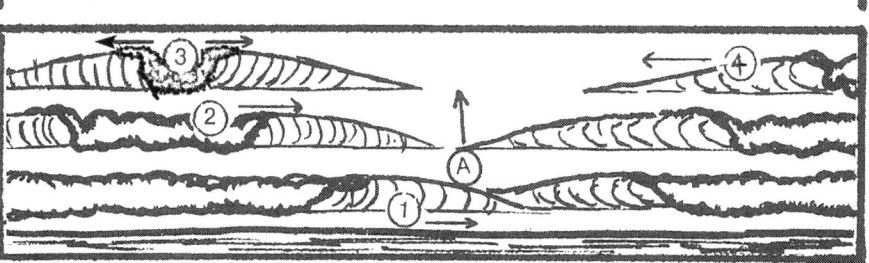

BEACH BREAKS — form over shifting sand bars (1) left shore break (2) middle break (3) outside peak & take off (4) right peak (A) paddle route between peaks.

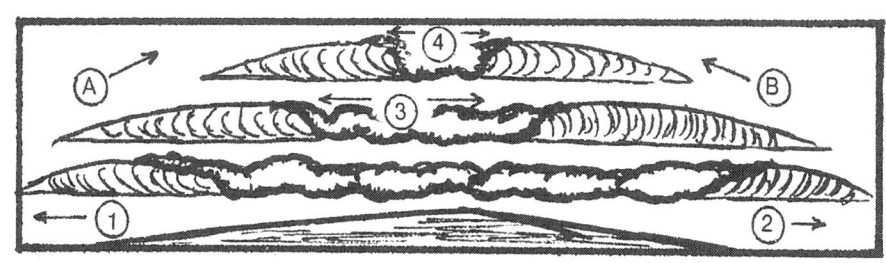

REEF BREAKS — form over submerged reefs (1) right shore break (2) left shore break (3) middle break (4) outside peak & take off (A&B) paddle routes around peak.

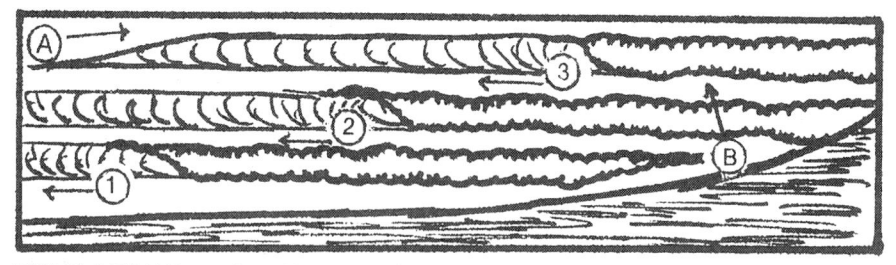

POINT BREAKS — form in cove of point (1) inside line up (2) middle break (3) outside line up & take off (A) inside paddle around line up (B) outside paddle through break.

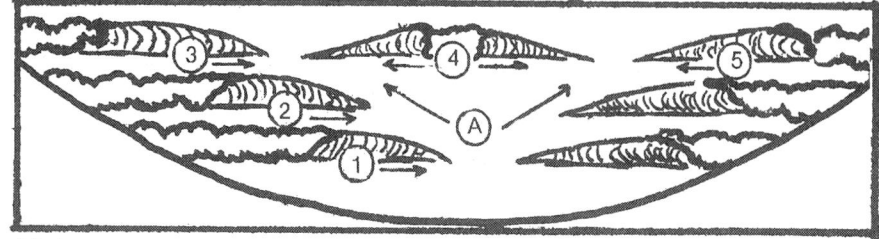

COVE BREAKS — form along both sides of cove & in middle reefs. (1) left shore break (2) middle break (3) left take off (4) reef break (5) right break (A) paddle through channels.

Beaches, Points & Reefs

Many reef breaks are accompanied by cliffs, kelp and canyon wind conditions. These conditions can contribute to making reef breaks surfable all day long and protect them from the prevailing on-shore winds. Reef breaks are also notorious for supporting the world's largest waves. Just remember that a reef break that looks like it is breaking one hundred feet from shore in three foot waves, may actually be breaking a half-mile out in twelve foot waves. The distance can be deceiving. But a small, close reef can provide excellent surfing for novices.

POINT BREAKS form in the cove of the point of land jutting out into the ocean. The waves form in long lines that wrap around the point and curl from the outside of the point clear into the cove. This lining-up formation of the wave around the point provides some of the longest quality rides to be found in surfing. Most experienced surfers watch their favorite point break like hawks, waiting for the right swell. The novice is usually stuck with in-between days or with finding his own secret point break.

Point breaks can break equally well at high tide or low tide and usually have some protection from the on-shore winds. Therefore, during a good swell, they can break excellent all day long, for days on end. Almost all point breaks have a rock bottom, which can make for painful walks after a lost board. This can be best handled with care in your surfing or tennis shoes on your feet. But the major menace would be the crowds at a point break which provide mainly a "one surfer wave," and every surfer in the water will be competing to be that one surfer. Stay clear of the major point breaks during big swells and find some minor ones that you can enjoy to yourself.

A COVE BREAK at its best can be like two point breaks with a left break off one side of the cove and a right break off the other. Sometimes you even get a reef break thrown into the middle as an added attraction. But don't worry too much about this situation, because it doesn't happen that often. At any rate, the cove usually comes accompanied by cliffs, kelp and canyon wind conditions and all day surfing.

A cove break would have many of the same requirements for a reef break, and would be most likely to break good at low tide. A cove break, along with reefs and points will break at their best only on the larger more defined swells of a season. Beach breaks, on the other hand, can break good on swells formed almost overnight by local wind conditions. For the best evaluation of when to surf a particular location, look at it. If it looks good, then is the time to surf it. This basic rule should guide to some excellent surfing.

JETTIES, PIERS & RIVER MOUTHS

Beneath each jetty, pier, river mouth, rock pile, inlet, sand spit, etc., you will find the basic bottom structure of a beach break, reef break or a point break. Below are different situations and how the surf may form around them.

ROCK JETTIES usually break something like a point break, if they break at all. Most jetties are very temperamental with their surf, requiring perfect tides, exact swell directions and no wind to break rideable. At high tide, most jetties will appear to break like a badly formed shore break. When the tide goes out, the jetty will play a major role in affecting the waves to curl evenly off the end of the jetty toward the beach.

Jetty waves are usually "one surfer waves" with very little extra room on the face of the wave for more than one surfer. Thus a jetty break may have the unique quality of being crowded with five people in the water. However, the novice may find his own secret jetty to afford him many hours of private surfing enjoyment.

FISHING PIERS have a way of doing nothing for the surfing line-up but forming an obstacle in the middle of the ride. Sometimes, the presence of a pier will make the sand bar formation of a beach break a little more pronounced and therefore create the best waves on a given beach. Novice surfers may find themselves faced with the challenge of "shooting the pier." They may also take off on a wave ready to shoot the pier and find that they have remarkable powers for instant re-evaluation as they approach the pier.

Actually shooting a pier can be quite easy, as most fishing piers form a deeper channel causing the wave to slow down through the pier. Most fishing piers break like a standard beach break with all the accompanyng tide and wind requirements. Novices who wish to test their surfing nerve and board strength may find surfing through piers to be most exhilirating.

AMUSEMENT PIERS may have much more effect on the surf because of the amount of closely spaced piling and the sand formations that build up as a result. This can make for excellent point-break type waves and a very high mortality rate for your surfboard, should you lose it. Most amusement piers do their best work on waves at low tide, when the sand bars have more effect. The thickest of pilings may also have a major effect in blocking the wind and allowing these locations to be ridable when other surf spots are blown out.

JETTIES, PIERS & RIVER MOUTHS

ROCK JETTY — forms cove-like point break (1) inside line-up (2) middle break (3) outside line-up and take off (A) inside paddle (B) paddle around jetty.

FISHING PIERS — may be right in surfing line up (1) shore break (2) middle break approaching pier (3) outside peak and take off (4) another peak (A&B) paddle routes.

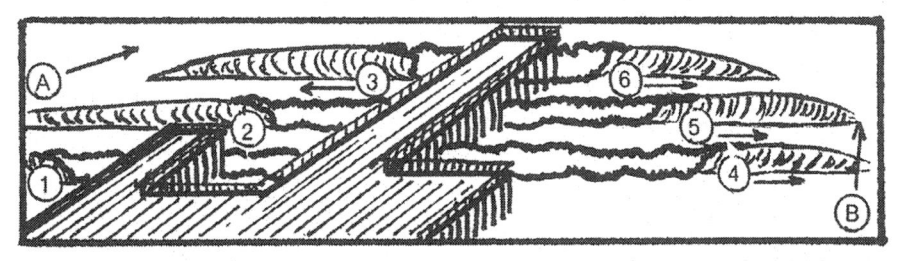

AMUSEMENT PIERS — may form point breaks (1) right shore break (2) middle break (3) right peak and take off (4) left shore break (5) middle break (6) left take off (A&B) paddles.

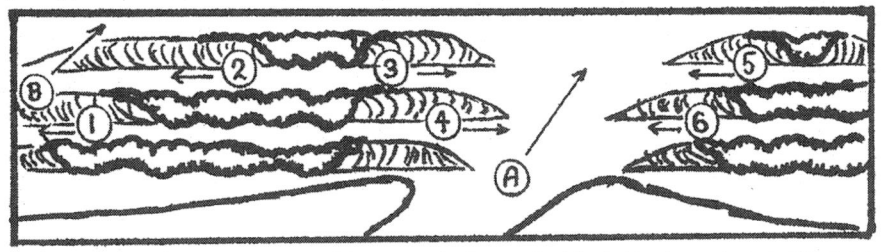

RIVER MOUTHS — form sand bars and channels (1) right shore break (2) right take off (3) hollow left take off (4) inside left (5) right peak and take off (6) inside right (A) river channel and paddle (B) paddle around line up.

Surf Breaks . . .

Surf breaks around natural and man made formations.

Large swells wrap around the point at Rincon.

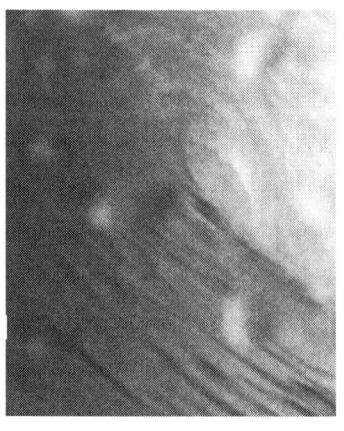

Good place to put your surfboard. Way before Go-Pro, maybe the first movies filmed from inside the tube. "The Living Curl" circa 1963.

With the right sand bars and wind direction, any beach can have perfect shaped waves.

Images from Jamie Budge's

The now defunct P.O.P. pier offered perfect rights of the south side, and perfect lefts off the north side. When the tide, swell and wind was right.

BACKWASH WAVES can launch body boards, skim boards and brave board surfers high into the air.

Once the wind comes up onshore, most perfect surf spots get blown to un-ridable chop. These days, short boarders use the choppy sections to launch airborne antics.

"The Living Curl" and "The Californians"

83

Jettiies, Piers & River Mouths

A novice should be somewhat wary of these types of pier break waves because they can be very unpredictable as they approach the pier. A pier wave may build up, flatten out, shelve and throw out in unexpected looping tubes as it hits different sand bar formations. As the loss of surfboard in this case may provide the surfer with two very short surfboards with barnacle dings, the novice should be most careful.

RIVER MOUTHS can also provide excellent and most challenging surfing breaks. The sand formations caused by the river emptying into the ocean may be very pronounced, resulting in super hollow "pipe-line" type peaks. These grinding peaks combined with the unpredictable river currents for most exciting surfing.

River mouths can be good at either high or low tide, but are very susceptible to on-shore winds. Even the slightest winds may cause these hollow waves to be most difficult to ride. Therefore, most river mouths are good early in the morning, during off-shore wind conditions or during all-day glass-offs. Novices riding river mouths should be strong paddlers and swimmers to be able to handle the difficult waves and pulling currents.

HARBOR & RIVER ENTRANCES can provide excellent and varied surfing if you can find a harbor or river that isn't constantly being dredged of all forming sandbars (in order to let those annoying boats through). The surf in these situations will usually be of a unique large rolling swell type of wave similar to the Waikiki surf. The actual break of the wave will be of little or no consequence and may sort of 'feather' down the face. Rather than "shooting the curl" or trimming across the face, the surfer will merely ride with the swell, sharing the wave with the rest of the small boats in the area.

Most harbor and river entrances will only break at extremely low tides and on large swells before the authorities decide it is time to dredge it again. Novices may find this kind of surf to be most enjoyable as well as affording excellent learning waves.

TIDES & SWELLS

The varying tide conditions play a major role in shaping the break of the wave. High tide, medium tide and low tide all have their distinct influence on the various locations.

HIGH TIDE causes the surf at most locations to break close in to the beach. At high tide, the swells are usually very thick, break with a lot of forward power, but do not form hollow tunnels as they break. Rides are usually shortest at high tide, with some rides ending right on the sand. Backwash (a wave forming back toward the surf from a steep beach) may cause mid-air surf antics as backwash and surf collide.

Some beach breaks may be best at high tide, particularly those with not too pronounced sand bar formations. Some beaches may break on entirely different sand bars at high tide than at low. Point breaks at high tide will also break close in to the sand. Rides may be shorter and crowds condensed. Waves may be lumpish and swelling with un-passable sections. Reef breaks at high tide may not break at all, due to the deep water over the reef. If they do break, it will be mostly a ride-with-the-swell situation with a feathering break.

MEDIUM TIDE will add a little zest to the sluggish breaks of high tide. Waves will be breaking out farther, with longer rides and hollower tubes. The crowds will be able to disperse a little, and new breaks may start forming with the dropping tide.

Beach breaks may develop their best possible waves as the outgoing tide puts sand bars at the perfect depth for excellent breaking peaks. Point breaks will start to line up better and those unmakable sections will start to open up into hollow fast spots. Reef breaks will start to develop some speed to the swelling action and some tube to the break.

LOW TIDE will turn some surfing locations into superbly breaking perfection waves, and turn others into junk. Waves will be breaking very far out in thin swells, long lines and hollow peeling tubes. Some beach breaks will be completely closing out in un-ridable surf, and others will be forming hollow peaks over outside sand bars. Rides will be longer and waves may form and re-form in different breaks. Point breaks can reach a perfection in peeling tunnels that is sought after by surfers throughout the world. Rides may be extremely long with several distinct breaks adding to the challenge. Reef breaks will be showing their best as swells hit submerged reefs and throw out in thin hollow tunnels. Take-offs may be a challenge just to get down the face of the wave before the tube takes you with it.

TIDES & SWELLS

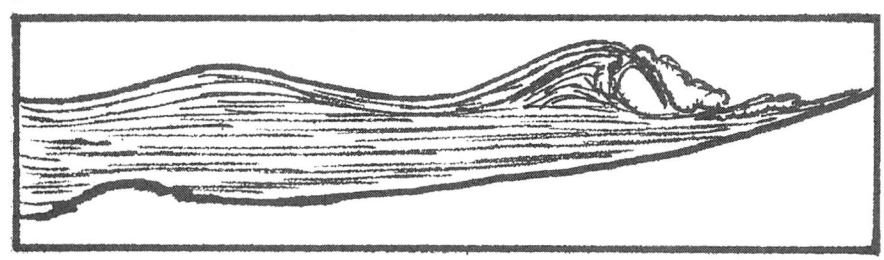

HIGH TIDE — Deep water, surf breaks close to shore line in thick swells. Rides are usually shorter and closer to the beach. Swells are not affected by outside reef.

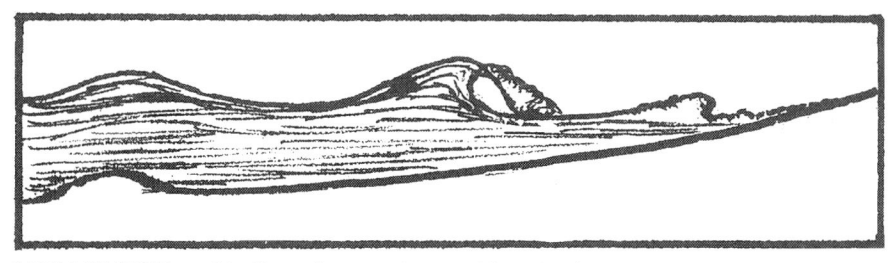

MEDIUM TIDE — Medium deep water surf breaks farther out with not so thick swells. Waves may be steeper, longer for faster rides. Swells beginning to hump on outside reef.

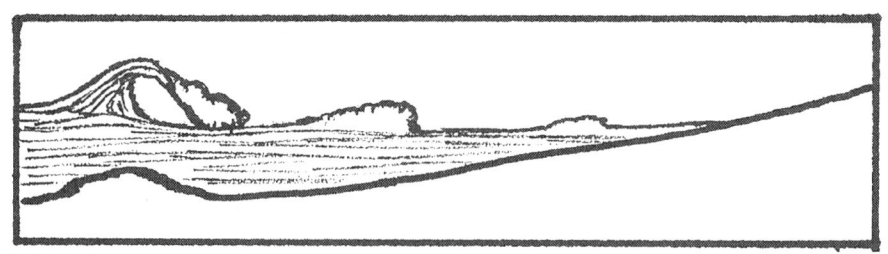

LOW TIDE — Shallow water, surf breaks far from beach in thin hollow swells. Waves may be throwing out in thin tunnels as swells break over outside reef for long rides.

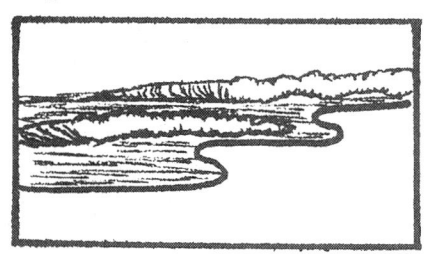

HIGH TIDE at a point break, thick swells break close to sandy beach.

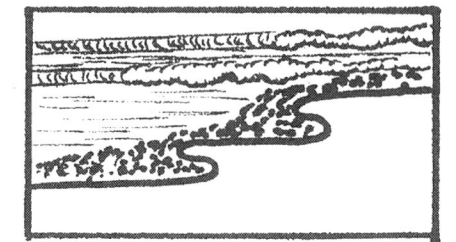

LOW TIDE at a point break, rocks exposed and swells breaking outside in long lines.

Tides & Swells

Low tide will expose rock formations and tideline flora and fauna for many yards between the high tide line and low tide water level. The time difference between high tide and low tide is a little less than six hours between each complete change. High tide, and low tide will occur approximately one hour later each day. Local tide tables can be consulted for exact tide changes.

WEATHER AND WAVES

The primary weather element affecting surf is the wind. Almost all waves are caused by wind conditions (except occasional earthquake waves). Distant storms will cause big surf in long, even lines. Local winds will cause "wind swell" surf which is smaller, peakier and less even in line-up. As these waves reach local surfing locations, again the wind is a primary element shaping the break of these waves.

Glassy conditions means no wind. This is the standard for best surfing conditions. The water is smooth, the face of the breaking wave is smooth and maneuvering is unrestricted. The line-up of the wave is well-defined, the curl will peel most evenly across the face and the shape of the wave will be dependent only on the bottom conditions and tide levels.

Off-shore winds mean that the winds blow against the face of the wave. This can be one of the most exciting of surfing conditions because the wind will hold the face of the wave up till the last possible second before it curls over in a tubing hollow break. Off-shore waves can also be difficult to surf because the wind blowing against the wave may make dropping into the wave and maneuvering a struggle against the force of the wind. The face of the wave may have a ripply surface chop which can also hamper maneuvering. But the large tunnels and the even line-ups caused by the wind can turn even the most mediocre surf spots into surfing perfection.

On-shore winds, on the other hand, ruin surf. Blowing from the ocean, these cause chop and turn perfection peeling waves into a crumbly mess. Most surfers do not like on-shore winds. The term accompanying on-shore winds is "Blown Out." It indicates a period of waiting for the conditions to get better. Canyon wind conditions can save some surf spots from on-shore winds and being blown out. A canyon in front of a surfing location may cause the normal on-shore winds to funnel off-shore out of the canyon mouth and make for good surfing conditions.

WEATHER & WAVES

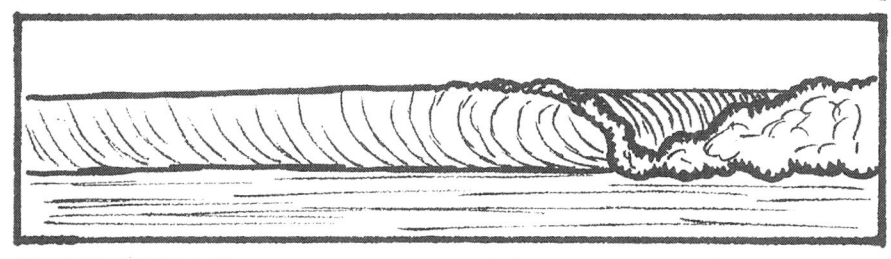

GLASSY CONDITIONS — No wind and smooth silky water. Waves break evenly in well defined lines with fast moving curl. Considered to be best conditions for surfing.

OFF SHORE CONDITIONS — Wind blows directly against waves blowing plumes of water off the curl. Waves break evenly with break holding up in wind. Exciting and challenging.

ON SHORE WIND CONDITIONS — Surf "blown out" by wind from the ocean causing chop and broken line-up of surf. Settle for bumpy uneven riding or go sailing.

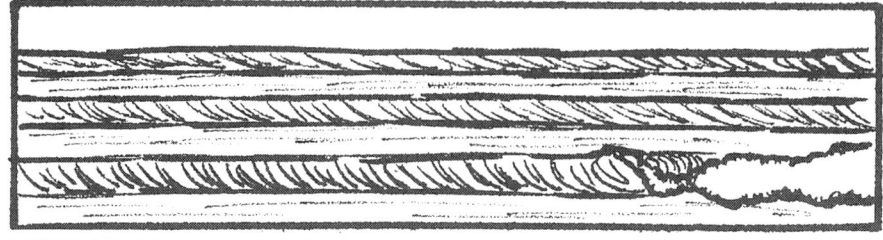

AFTER STORM CONDITIONS — Surf is "UP" from distant storms causing long large lines of surf to pour through at favorite surfing locations.

Weather & Waves

Rain can many times accompany good surfing conditions. The storms may bring in the rain along with the large waves. The rainy conditions may also bring about an all-day glass-off or off-shore winds which can both be good for surfing. On the other hand, a good rain-storm may also bring "victory at sea" for several days till the ocean calms down enough from very rough conditions, to be ridable again.

Heat spells, unfortunately, are many times accompanied by flat surf (no surf). This is because the local doldrum also indicates a lack of the necessary wave-creating wind at sea. The perfect combination would be a distant tropical storm combined with a local hot spell. The result could be large surf, warm weather and glassy conditions. And everybody and his little brother out riding the surf. The trick is to find when the right combination of weather, waves, tides and lack of crowds come together for the excellent surfing experience.

SEASONS AND SURF

Every surfing location, or surfing area has its best season. This is a combination of time of year and the direction of the swell. In the winter, the swells will come from the north and from storms in the northern hemisphere and in the Aleutian Islands. Because of the basic angle of each surfing location bottom formation, some spots will break excellent on a north swell and some spots will not break at all. This is especially true of point breaks and reef breaks, which will have the most pronounced and permanent angle in relationship to the swell direction. Many points and reefs that break during the winter will not break at all during the summer.

Most large summer swells come from tropical storms in the southern hemisphere and miss the angle for breaking correctly at winter locations. And many summer points and reefs will not break at all during the winter. Most beach breaks will catch both a north and a south swell but will break a little differently on each. And most surfing locations will have a month or two out of the year when they are expected to be supreme: when all the conditions of weather, tides, winds, swell directions and bottom formations will come together for the best that a particular surfing spot has to offer. Most local surfers have their areas completely wired in this way, and will be glad to tell any novice outsider the exact opposite of what actually goes on at his particular surfing location.

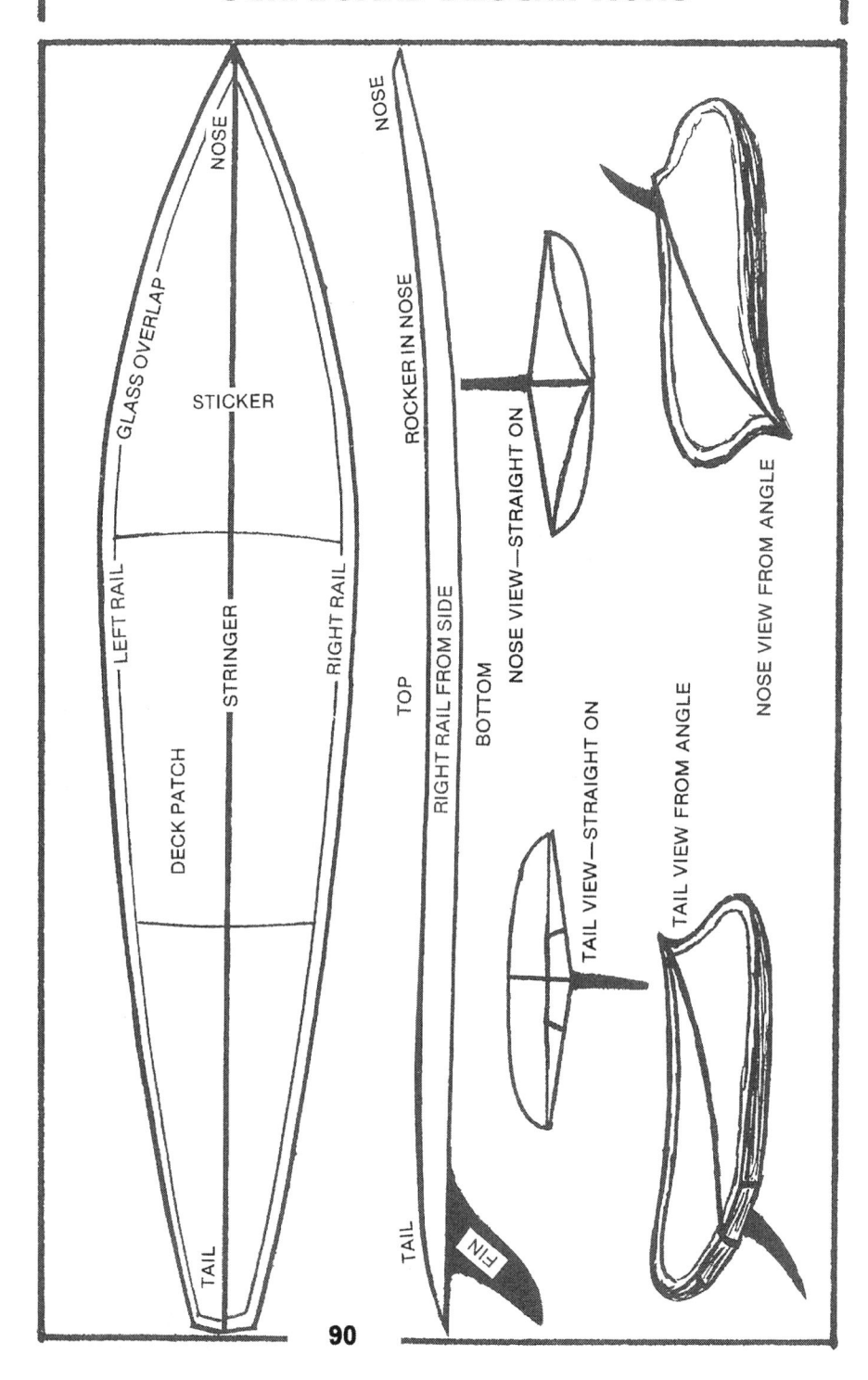

SURFBOARD DESCRIPTIONS

SURFBOARD DESCRIPTIONS

The terminology involved in describing a surfboard is somewhat necessary for the survival of the novice in the world of surfboard sales. Without some sort of advance study, it is possible for the board salesman to give a very convincing pitch for a certain style board without the novice ever understanding a word of what the salesman is talking about. Below are the obvious terms involved in describing a surfboard:

Deck — the top of a board.

Bottom — the bottom of a board.

Rail — the edge of a board.

Deck Patch — an extra layer of fibreglass cloth on the deck of the board (to protect it from the extra weight of the surfer).

Nose — the front of the board.

Tail — the back end of the board.

Stringer — the wooden, foam or glass strip down the center of the board.

Rocker — the curve in the deck of a surfboard.

Fin — the fin on the bottom tail of the board (sometimes called a skeg).

Plan shape — the design of the board from the top.

Rail lines — the design of the board from the edge.

Surfboards are usually described in terms of length, width and thickness, when referring to the plan shape, the rail lines and different parts of the board. Surfboards are mostly made of plastic foam, presently, with wooden stringers and covered with fibreglass cloth and resin.

Blanks are unshaped blocks of foam. The blanks are shaped to a certain design by a surfboard shaper who shapes with electric planers and sanding blocks. These shaped foam blanks are then glassed by a glasser who cuts the fibreglass cloth to size and then pours on mixed resin and catalyst to make a complete fibreglass coating. This fibreglass is then coated with a fill coat of resin and sanded to perfection smoothness and design by a sander with an electric sander. The board is then glossed with a final coat of resin applied by brush, and polished with an electric polisher. Color is sometimes added to the fibreglass cloth or the final coats of glossing resin. The entire process of manufacturing a surfboard can be easily completed within a few days. However, because of production techniques to handle several boards at one time, usual delivery time is about two to three weeks.

Surfboard Designs . . .

Whatever the size or shape, it's important to bring as many as possible.

These days, surfboards seem to fit into two major classifications:
LONG (8 to 11 ft) and SHORT (5 to 6 ft).
And dozens (if not hundreds) of sub-catagories

Consult your local surf shop (or surfers on the beach) for popular favorites.

92   Images from Jamie Budge's "The Californians".

SURFBOARD DESIGN

There are as many subtle designs in the shapes of surfboards as there are in the shapes of girls. With surfboards, each shape is designed for a certain type of performance in a certain kind of wave or surf situation. Most designs are carefully shaped in several generations and tested over and over in different surfing situations for which they were designed. Below are some of the characteristics of the most popular designs:

GUN SHAPE — sometimes called big gun or semi-gun or baby gun depending on the extreme of the design. Guns are designed primarily for surf ranging from large to super scary heavy big. Guns usually range from about 8 ft. to 9 ft. in length and can be a narrow 16 inches to 18 in width. The bottom or rail design of a gun is extremely important to insure proper control of the forces of larger surf. The rails are usually down hard with a hard or sharp rail for carving and holding on the face of a large wave. A "V" bottom in the tail can give extra plow or speed to turns.

STANDARD SHAPE — designed for California surf and smaller island surf. The "Standard" shape leaves a lot of variables in the designs used for a medium sized, medium powerful wave. A standard shape usually ranges from about 7 ft. to 8 ft. in length, and is about 18½ to 19½ inches wide. The rails may be down hard in the tail but softer toward the middle and the nose. A "V" bottom in the tail may be standard on the standard.

RADICAL MANEUVERING SHAPE — is designed for a lot of radical turning on small surf. This type board may be out of control in medium surf and launched into outer space by really large surf. A radical maneuver board may be a shorter 6 ft. to 7 ft. in length and a wider 19 to 20 inches in width. The rails may be full and hard down for flotation and radical carving on the face of the wave. The bottom may be absolutely flat or concave to increase this tight carving ability.

BEGINNING BOARDS — are designed to make learning easier for the novice and beginning sufers. They work good in smaller easier breaking waves and have extra flotation and stability. A beginning board my be a slightly longer 7½ to 8½ ft. long and a wider 19 inches to 20 inches in width. These boards are generally thicker for flotation and have soft rounded rails for easy unrestricted turning. The nose and tail are usually wider for stability. A "V" bottom may add to the flotation and easy turning.

OTHER DESIGNS — include:

Nose Riders — with flat noses or concave noses for longer, more stable nose rides.

Twin Fin designs, for radical maneuvers on extremely small surf.

Rail Fins — for extra carve on radical turns.

SURFBOARD DESIGNS

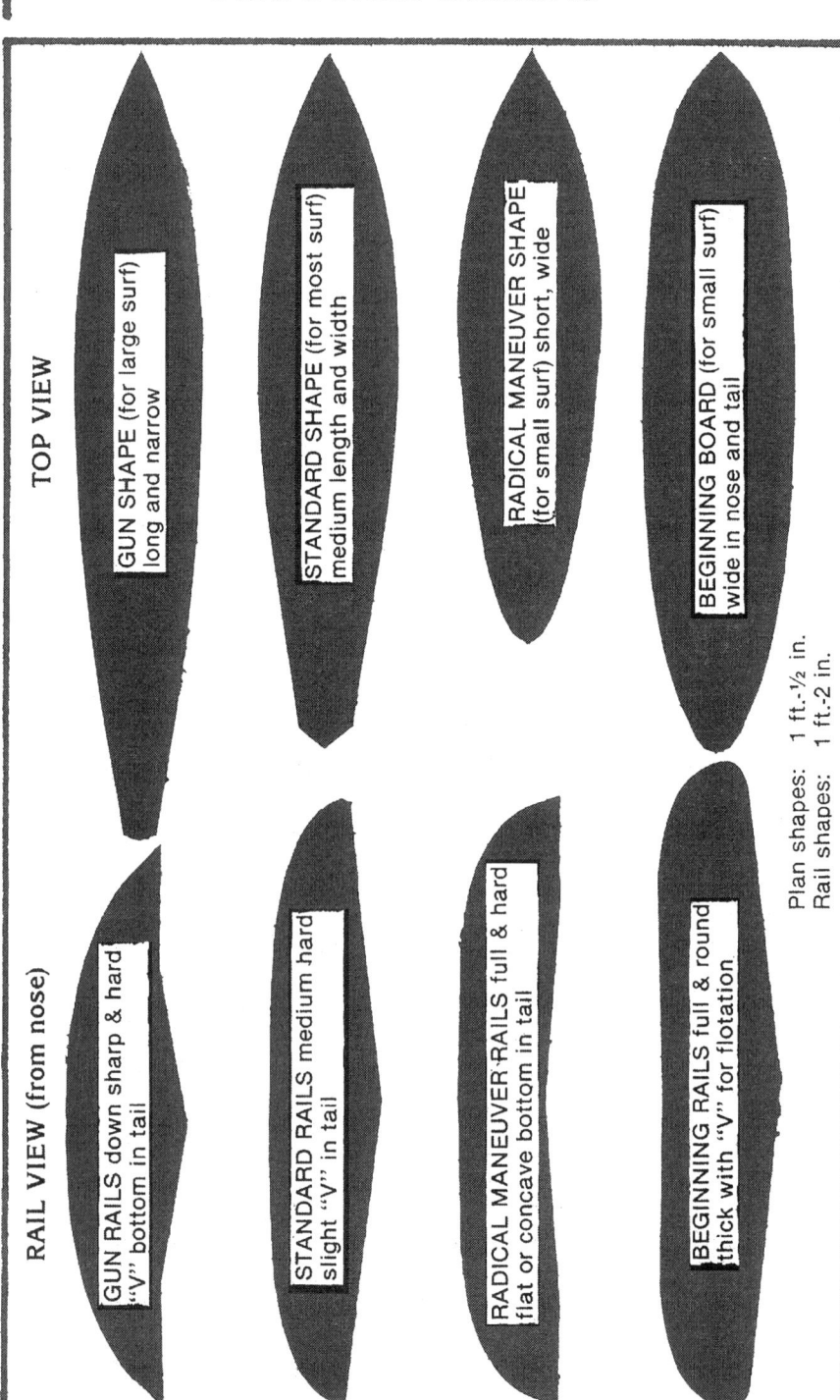

TOP VIEW

- **GUN SHAPE** (for large surf) long and narrow
- **STANDARD SHAPE** (for most surf) medium length and width
- **RADICAL MANEUVER SHAPE** (for small surf) short, wide
- **BEGINNING BOARD** (for small surf) wide in nose and tail

RAIL VIEW (from nose)

- **GUN RAILS** down sharp & hard "V" bottom in tail
- **STANDARD RAILS** medium hard slight "V" in tail
- **RADICAL MANEUVER RAILS** full & hard flat or concave bottom in tail
- **BEGINNING RAILS** full & round thick with "V" for flotation

Plan shapes: 1 ft.-½ in.
Rail shapes: 1 ft.-2 in.

Surfboard Designs

Super Scoops — rocker in the nose for nose rides.
Slot Bottoms — for extra draw on the turns.
Swallow Tails — for draw in turning on larger waves.
Pin Tails — for stability and carve on large waves.
Step Decks — for focused and reduced flotation.
Square Rails or Diamond Rails — for accentuated turning.
And assorted other concoctions for the advancement or confusion of current popular surfboard designs.

The size of a surfboard that a surfer should buy is sort of a relative thing, depending on the style and design of his board, how much he weighs and the type of waves he wishes to ride. Some estimations on what a surfer might ride are listed below:

A 125 lb. surfer might ride a 7 ft. Beginning Board, a 6 ft. 2 in. Radical Maneuver Board, a 6 ft. 8 in. Standard and a 7 ft. 2 in. Gun.

A 150 lb. surfer might ride a 7 ft. 6 in. Beginning Board, a 6 ft. 6 in. Radical Maneuver Board, a 7 ft. 6 in. Standard Shape and an 8 ft. Gun.

A 175 lb. surfer might ride a 7 ft. 9 in. Beginning Board, a 6 ft. 9 in. Radical Maneuver Board, a 7 ft. 6 in. Standard Shape and an 8 ft. 4 in. Gun.

A 200 lb. surfer might ride an 8 ft. Beginning Board, a 7 ft. Radical Maneuver Board, an 8 ft. Standard Shape and a 9 ft. Gun.

These estimates are somewhat arbitrary, as the lengths may vary as much as one foot in any direction depending on local tastes or current trends. Local surf shops are usually the best consultants on what is currently popular and best suited to an individual's needs for where he is going to surf.

SURFBOARDS
Transport, Care and Repair

The methods of adapting your surfboard to your car (or your car to your surfboard) are numerous. The most universal method for almost any car is the surfboard rack which fits on top of the car by clamping onto the raingutter moulding. These racks will normally hold up to four boards comfortable and up to eight boards in various stages of precariousness. Aside from the racks, there are various methods to fit different surfboards inside the cars.

Each surfboard or car will require a different combination of ingenuity. In some cars a longer board might fit out the back window, with shorter boards it might fit completely in the back of the car. There are also certain combinations of folding down the front seat on the passenger's side and placing one board next to the driver. In busses or vans, boards can be merely placed in back or hung inside from racks built next to the roof of the van.

Almost any method is acceptable except the dangerous ones. Don't, for instance, tie or set boards on top of the car without the aid of a rack. Boards secured (?) in this manner have a way of coming off and blowing down the highway into oncoming traffic. This can be most unfortunate for your board. Don't stick your board sideways out a window where passing cars, bicycles or policeman may pick it off. Don't tie or hold your board to the side on the car or allow it to protrude beyond the dimensions of the car without a flag, or outside local vehicle restrictions. Also don't put the board inside the car where it will decapitate drivers or passengers, should the car come to an abrupt halt.

Taking care of your board consists primarily of not leaving it for prolonged periods of time in the hot sun. This can cause the board to discolor, the fibreglass to become brittle and sometimes the foam to swell or expand. By setting your board for a short time in the sun, deck up, the wax will melt and allow you to scrape it off and start over with clean wax. Dirt, old wax, smears and smudges may be further removed with acetone or lacquer thinner.

The main concern for the upkeep of a surfboard is the recurrence of dings (which are dents and breaks in the glass and foam caused by collisions with rock, piers and other surfboards.)These dings can be temporarily sealed with plastic tape to keep them water tight. But a permanent repair should be made as soon as possible.

TRANSPORT, CARE & REPAIR OF SURFBOARDS

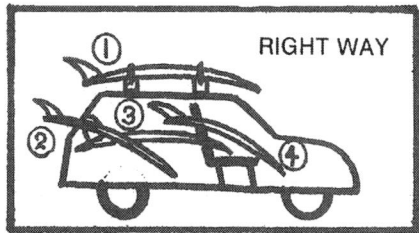

RIGHT WAY

WRONG WAY

BOARD TRANSPORTATION (1) on rack (2) out back (3) in back (4) over front seat.

DON'T (1) tie boards without rack (2) stick out side (3) tie to side (4) put on driver.

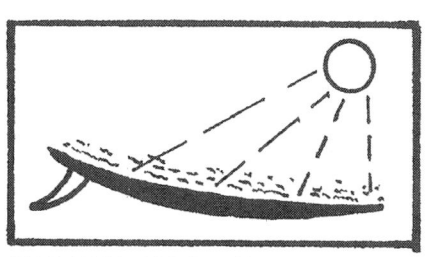

WAX WILL MELT off board in sun. Clean board with acetone or lacquer thinner.

PLASTIC TAPE will temporarily seal ding from water.

FIX DING — file away torn glass and foam.

POUR PUTTY and mould to fill hole in board. Sand smooth.

FIBREGLASS CLOTH & RESIN will cover entire damaged area.

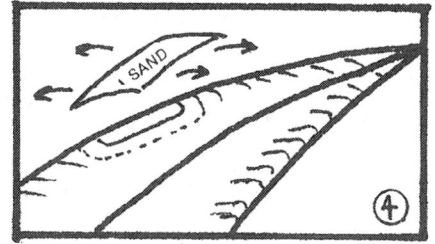

SAND SMOOTH to match board contours. Gloss with final coat of resin.

Surfboard Repair

Dings are repaired by first filing away old damaged glass and foam. This should leave the ding clean and dry. Small dings can then be repaired with a putty mixture of resin (and catalyst) plus baking flour or a commercial putty mix. This is mixed to desired thickness and applied to fill the hole. When it dries, it is sanded smooth and glossed with a final coat of clear resin. With bigger dings, a block of foam may be required to fill the hole. This block is fitted to size and resined into place. The foam or putty is then sanded to fit the contours of the board, and then to a level below flush with the contours, to leave room for the fibreglass to fill.

The fibreglass cloth is then cut to the shape of the ding and mixed resin is poured onto the cloth. This is worked to cover all the ding and sanded area and bring the contours back up to flush with the rest of the lines of the board. When the cloth dries, a fill coat of resin is applied to fill the natural weave of the cloth. When this dries, the entire area is sanded smooth to match the exact contours of the lines of the board and a final coat of resin is brushed on to seal the area, and finish the job. Fibreglass materials for repairing surfboards are available at surf shops, plastics stores and paint stores. These will come with instructions for the appropriate mixtures of resin, catalysts and drying times. For small dings, the amounts of catalyst may be increased to speed up the drying or hardening time.

WETSUITS, CARE AND REPAIR

Wetsuits are the primary salvation to surfing in cold weather and water. Without them, surfing can become uncomfortable or impossible in many areas during colder parts of the year. Wetsuits should be chosen to fit tightly, to insure warmth from body heat that is transferred to the thin layer of water between the suit and your body. If the wetsuit is too loose, the layer of water will be running in and out and be as cold as the outside temperatures. But the wetsuit should not restrict arm movement, inhibit breathing or cause chapping at any tender spots. Should chapping occur (usually under the arms, from paddling) vaseline can be applied to alleviate the rubbing.

Wetsuits should not be left out in the sun for any length of time as this will cause the rubber to shrink, harden and become brittle. After each day of surfing, it is best to wash your wetsuit out in clear water to remove the salt deposits which will also deteriorate the rubber.

WETSUITS—CARE & REPAIR

CHOOSE WETSUIT that fits tight but does not restrict arm movement (or breathing).

WASH WETSUIT in clear water after using to rinse off salt from ocean.

DO NOT LEAVE IN SUN for any length of time. Sun will shrink rubber and make brittle.

VASOLINE will alleviate chapping from rubbing against wetsuit.

FIX TEARS IN WETSUIT when clean and dry. Apply glue to both sides of tear and let dry.

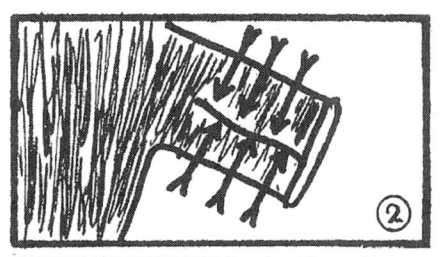

PRESS TOGETHER both sides of tear after second coat has dried about five minutes.

SEW TOGETHER sides of tear after gluing. Use thick dacron thread and needle.

FINAL COAT of glue will cover stitching and seal repair work.

Wetsuit Repair

Should a tear or rip develop in your wetsuit, it is best to fix it before it lengthens. Clean and dry the wetsuit and tear. Apply black cement (designed for wetsuits) to both sides of the tear. Allow to dry for five minutes. Re-apply a second coat of black cement after the first has dried. Allow this to dry for about five minutes. Then press together both sides of the tear and the contact action of the cement will adhere them together.

The tear can then be stitched for further strength in the repair. This is done with a thicker dacron thread and needle. The stitches should be far enough apart to leave plenty of rubber to hold the stitches, or they will rip out. A final coat of cement will cover the stitches and seal the repair work. The black rubber cement is available at many skin diving shops and surf shops with complete instructions on how to use the cement, along with drying times necessary.

COLORFUL SURFING TERMINOLOGY

Avalanche — refers to a lot of water breaking down the face of a wave, usually a large one.
Baby gun — a surfboard designed for baby heavy waves, as in semi-gun or big gun.
Backside — riding with back to the wave.
Bar — usually refers to a sand formation under the water.
Beach — sandy place next to ocean.
Big gun — a surfboard designed for big heavy waves.
Black magic — wetsuit cement (black in color).
Blown out — surf blown choppy by on-shore wind.
Board — that foam and fibreglass thing that you bought with this book.
Bombers — hard breaking waves.
Bottom turn — a turn off the bottom of the wave.
Bowl — section of wave hollowed out in the form of a bowl, as the "Makaha Bowl."
Camper — fits on back of pick-up truck to hold more surfboards.
Carve — to bank or slice across the face of a wave.
Catalyst — makes resin harden.
Climb and drop — two things a surfer does to go up and down across the face of a wave.

Colorful Surfing Terminology

Close out — a wave that breaks all at once with no surfers direction.
Concave — hollowed out tail or nose of a surfboard. Usually on bottom.
Curl — breaking part of the wave.
Cut back — a turn back toward the break of the wave.
"Da Cat" — extremely agile animal noticed roaming Malibu beaches.
Deck — top of surfboard or place by pool.
Deck patch — extra layer of fibreglass on top of board.
Diamond — a rail or tail, (or a thing a surfer wishes he could find in the sand.)
Dings — those little holes that you find on your board after losing it on the rocks.
Drive — a surfboard as in car. With speed and direction.
Egg rails — rounded easy rails mostly on beginning boards.
Face — front of the wave.
Falls — is in "over the _____," referes to the breaking lip of the wave.
Flat — no surf, when referring to waves.
Fly-away — pull-out maneuver or constant struggle on hot sandy beach.
Fin — that thing sticking out of the bottom of your board.
Fin release — surfing maneuver where fin slides sideways down wave.
Fibreglass — the outside stuff your board is made out of.
Foam — the inside stuff your board is made out of.
Glass — fibreglass.
Goofy foot — surfer who rides right foot forward.
Green room — the tunnel of the wave.
Ground swell — sort of funny swell condition between wind swell and storm swell.
Gun — big wave board.
Hang five — five toes over the nose of the board.
Hang ten — ten toes over the nose of the board.
Hard — sharp rails on a surfboard.
Head dip — sticking your head in the wave.
Heavy — big wave or latest hard rock record.
Hollow — wave breaking in a big loop.
Hot-dogger — that guy who sells lunch on the board walk.
Islands — usually refers to those popular ones in the middle of the Pacific.

Colorful Surfing Terminology

Inside — as in the tube, or inside of a large set of waves or the inside line-up.
Jeep — good vehicle for rides on a ranch.
Jetty — that pile of rocks going out in the middle of your beach.
Kickout — to get you and your board out of a wave.
Knee action — skiing style of surfing.
Kuk — you, if you're just learning to surf.
Lean — as to lean in the direction of a turn.
Left — wave that breaks to the left.
Lip — breaking film of water.
Line-up — the way a wave breaks.
Lined-up — long lines of a wave.
Long board — 9 to 20 ft. in length.
Loop — the tube of a wave.
Loose — easy maneuvering surfboard.
Long John — coverall wetsuit.
Low tide — what do you say, the opposite of high tide.
Mush — extremely slow easy breaking surf, may be good for learning.
Nose — front of the surfboard.
Nose ride — a ride on the front of the surfboard.
Off shore — a wind that blows off shore against the ocean and waves.
Off the lip — a surfing maneuver that takes the surfer up to the top of the break of the wave.
On shore — a wind that blows on shore from the ocean causing choppy conditions.
Outside — refers to waves forming outside of a particular position.
Over the falls — part of a wipe-out where the surfer gets sucked over with the break of the wave.
Paddle — what you do on your surfboard to get out to the surf.
Parallel stance — riding facing directly forward with one foot toward each rail. Can get extremely uncomfortable if one foot slips off.
Pier — that thing you don't want to lose your board into.
Peak — a wave that is shaped similar to its namesake in mountains.
Pig board — a fat sluggish board (good for mushy surf).
Pigment — stuff in your surfboard that makes it a color. Stuff in your skin that keeps you from sunburning.

Colorful Surfing Terminology

Plan shape — the way your board looks from the top.

Pipeline — a super hollow wave forming a "pipeline" or hollow between the breaking lip and the face of the wave.

Pocket — where you put your surfboard for a tube ride and your hand for your money.

Power surfer — one who surfs with power.

Rail — the edge of your surfboard.

Reef — mound of coral, rocks, old cars, etc. over which waves break.

Regular foot — stands on board with right foot forward.

Release — a sensation that a surfer gets after a thrilling wave or a bad experience in Tijuana.

Resin — gooey syrupy stuff that mixes with catalyst and pours on fibreglass cloth to make your surfboard.

Right — a direction of a breaking wave.

Ripples — a condition of surf that calls for a similarly named beverage.

Rivermouth — where river meets ocean.

"S" maneuver — turn back and bottom turn on waves or surfer on highway tyring to make up his mind which direction the surf is best.

Sand spit — small irregular formation of beach or what surfer does after face-down wipe-out in shallow sandy water.

Semi gun — a surfboard that is sort of shaped like a big gun.

Shape — usually used in reference to design of board or female participants.

Shelve — condition of bottom that causes wave to break unexpectedly.

Shop — the place where one buys surfboards and this book.

Shoulder — edge or easy part of wave where break is not difficult or hollow. Good place for kooks to get in the way of experienced surfers.

Skeg — or fin, not to be confused with rudder, keel, centerboard, aileron or any other incorrect references that have nothing to do with the thing sticking out of the bottom of a surfboard.

Soup — white water part of wave and supplement to surfers diet of beans.

Soft rails — design of beginners board or condition of rails with lots of dings.

Spinner — useless turn around on board with all the practicality of a headstand.

Colorful Surfing Terminology

Spring suit — wetsuit that a surfer wears in the spring (usually long sleeves and short legs).
Square rails — indicates radical design or lazy shaper.
Step deck — split level design of surfboard.
Spit — a blast of water blown out of the tube in a spray of water.
Stalling — maneuver on wave to slow speed.
Sticker — label on surfboard or car window.
Straight over — type of close-out surf (or how surfer falls after wild party).
Surf knots — calcium deposits on knees and feet caused by paddling surfboard on knees.
Swallow tail — design of surfboard named after design of bird.
Swell — wave before it breaks and condition of novice surfer's head as he begins to surf better.
Super — type of surf condition and grade of gasoline.
Tail — end of surfboard.
Take-off — beginning of ride.
Tandem — two people on one surfboard.
"Tight" — refers to close position on critical breaking wave.
Tracks — path of surfers' maneuvers across face of waves.
Trimming — position in surfing and the closest surfers ever come to a haircut.
Tube — hollow part of wave and rubber thing you float around on after "no surfing" signs go up.
Van — lots of room for surfboards and other activities.
Vaseline — gooey stuff to ease chapping of wet-suit.
Victory at sea — indicates rough conditions as in the beginning of popular TV series.
Wax — rub on surfboard for traction.
Wave hogs — as in "road hogs," one who hogs the wave.
Wedge — a bowling hollow section of wave.
Wind swell — surf condition caused by local winds.
Wipe-out — unpleasant end of the ride.
Woody — type of station wagon popular with early fadist surfers (refer to Beach Boys recordings).

What they're saying . . .

" . . . it is already my favorite surf movie in my entire collection, beyond my expectations. You captured that era in the early 60's (actually my era when I first got started), better than anyone had ever done before. I am also so impressed with your surfing ability and style way back then. You were actually as good as all those guys, ability and style, maybe a synthesis of everyone of those guys you featured."   Ira Nepus

More brilliance from Jamie Budge - the genius who brought us the masterpiece "The Living Curl"   John Hintlian

Your movies are selling like hot cakes!!! Marie, Tyler Surfboards

LOVE "The Californians" great historical content of the early '70's! Watched some of the new DVD tonight @ the HB Surf Museum with DAVID, classic early Seventies stuff about when I first landed on these shores in '72! Peter Townend

Jamie,   Watched your movie last night and thoroughly enjoyed it.   I especially like that you, were a fine surfer in your time, related properly to all of those guys and told us the real inside out of what was going on. Again, Jamie, I really enjoyed your unhurried narrative, and how you threaded the scenes together... giving me for one, memories of all those guys... especially those who I'd say were of the 'Slipcheck Era'   Aloha, tom (Morey, inventor of the Boogie Board and Slipcheck).

I gave a copy of "The Californians" to my friend Mike who shapes for Tyler. He particularly appreciated the part about the "dark days" of shaping when boards sucked. He said he has tried to explain that era to people and your movie totally nails it. Thank you Jamie.   Aloha,   Katherine and David Kramer

Hi Jamie, Yes, the film should sell itself. It is wonderful and I enjoyed every minute. Roger Mann, Longboard Collector Club

ON YOUR FILMS JAMIE. THANK YOU FOR YOUR PASSION IN ALLOWING OUR GENERATION AN APPRECIATION THROUGH FILM,   TO RECALL A WONDERFULL ERA. YOUR STYLE EXEMPLIFIES THAT PERIOD. CONTINUE GRININ & TRIMIN, SAF

Hi Jamie   Glad to see you are doing the dvds they really fill in a missing part of surfing history   Later Skip (Engblom)

"AWESOME! " The Californians" captures the essence of the culture & freedom of that innocent time, in addition to all the Amazing surfers, friends, & culture all rolled into one great film." Jan Bar

The Living Curl

Jamie Budge's Classic Surf Film from the Early Sixties

Featuring... Miki Dora, Johnny Fain, Lance Carson, Dewey Weber, Harold Iggy, Mike Doyle, Rusty Miller, John Peck, Rick Irons, Mark Martinson, Corky Carroll, David Nuuhiwa and more .... all in their prime !

thelivingcurl.com © jamiebudge@windskate.com

Trailers on youtube: "The Living Curl" "The Californians Surf"

Building Blocks of Modern Surfing
2 Great DVD's
1962 - 1965
1966 - 1974 +

Since his teens, Janie Budge surfed the beaches of Southern California. With his camera, he recorded surfing history as it unfolded in front of him.

Trailers on youtube: "The Living Curl" "The Californians Surf"

THE CALIFORNIANS

A "New" film from Jamie Budge

The Long and Short of it . . .

The Late '60's, early '70's were all about change: in society, our surfboards and the way we rode them. From the perspective of **"Four Years After"** you could see how far we had come. The best of the old. The newest of the "new".

Available from:
thelivingcurl.com jamiebudge@windskate.com
starrfilms.com starrphoto@barfoot.com

What they're saying . . .

Hi Jamie   Received your movie, The Californians, the other day..   Nice work.. Enjoyed it more than the first one.   Left me feeling good and proud to be part of that era.   We were lucky to have lived it.. And survived.   ALOHA Sparky Hudson

Watched it last night was every bit as good as living curl - which is one of my all time favorites. Stefanie Phillips

Jamie–   Stoked on your new film! I will unleash the Facebook hounds immediately! And I look forward to attending the premier!
Warm regards,   Glenn,   Liquid Salt Magazine   Profiles of the people who make the history, art and culture of surfing.

We are stoked to see the classic surfing of those golden times. aaron, surfindian

Niiiice Jamie!   Exciting! I just watched the trailer. Good stuff!   Julie Cox, California Surf Museum

Let's figure out a date to do an indoor screening of your latest movie, complete with you narrating it.   Barry Haun, Surfing Heritage Foundation

Hi Jamie   The premiere of your movie is now on our website. When you have DVDs available, let me know as we'd like some to sell as before.   All the best with the new one.   Regards   Mick McAuliffe, Pacific Longboarder

Of "The Living Curl" I wrote: "The Living Curl" is a "must see" for all those interested in surfing's rich history anyone wanting to enjoy a surfing film that combines all the elements needed to make it a classic."   Since I've run out of superlatives, the same can be said for "The Californians". It is really, really , REALLY GREAT! Robert Feigel   surfwriter.net   writer for '60's Surf Guide Magazine,

Best film I've never been in . . .   Meringue Keru

Trailers on youtube: "The Living Curl"   "The Californians Surf"

Printed in Great Britain
by Amazon